"This series is a tremendous resource for those wanting to study and teach the Bible with an understanding of how the gospel is woven throughout Scripture. Here are gospel-minded pastors and scholars doing gospel business from all the Scriptures. This is a biblical and theological feast preparing God's people to apply the entire Bible to all of life with heart and mind wholly committed to Christ's priorities."

BRYAN CHAPELL, pastor; author, *Christ-Centered Preaching* and *Christ-Centered Worship*

"Mark Twain may have smiled when he wrote to a friend, 'I didn't have time to write you a short letter, so I wrote you a long letter.' But the truth of Twain's remark remains serious and universal, because well-reasoned, compact writing requires extra time and extra hard work. And this is what we have in the Crossway Bible study series *Knowing the Bible*. The skilled authors and notable editors provide the contours of each book of the Bible as well as the grand theological themes that bind them together as one Book. Here, in a 12-week format, are carefully wrought studies that will ignite the mind and the heart."

R. KENT HUGHES, Senior Pastor Emeritus, College Church, Wheaton, Illinois

"*Knowing the Bible* brings together a gifted team of Bible teachers to produce a high-quality series of study guides. The coordinated focus of these materials is unique: biblical content, provocative questions, systematic theology, practical application, and the gospel story of God's grace presented all the way through Scripture."

PHILIP G. RYKEN, President, Wheaton College

"These *Knowing the Bible* volumes provide a significant and very welcome variation on the general run of inductive Bible studies. This series provides substantial instruction, as well as teaching through the very questions that are asked. *Knowing the Bible* then goes even further by showing how any given text links with the gospel, the whole Bible, and the formation of theology. I heartily endorse this orientation of individual books to the whole Bible and the gospel, and I applaud the demonstration that sound theology was not something invented later by Christians, but is right there in the pages of Scripture."

GRAEME L. GOLDSWORTHY, former lecturer in Old Testament, Biblical Theology, and Hermeneutics, Moore Theological College

"What a gift to earnest, Bible-loving, Bible-searching believers! The organization and structure of the Bible study format presented through the *Knowing the Bible* series is so well conceived. Students of the Word are led to understand the content of passages through perceptive, guided questions, and they are given rich insights and application all along the way in the brief but illuminating sections that conclude each study. What potential growth in depth and breadth of understanding these studies offer! One can only pray that vast numbers of believers will discover more of God and the beauty of his Word through these rich studies."

BRUCE A. WARE, T. Rupert and Lucille Coleman Professor of Christian Theology, The Southern Baptist Theological Seminary

T0341609

KNOWING THE BIBLE

Douglas Sean O'Donnell, Series Editor

• • • • • •

Genesis
Exodus
Leviticus
Numbers
Deuteronomy
Joshua
Judges
Ruth and Esther
1–2 Samuel
1–2 Kings
1–2 Chronicles
Ezra and Nehemiah
Job
Psalms
Proverbs

Ecclesiastes
Song of Solomon
Isaiah
Jeremiah
Lamentations, Habakkuk, and Zephaniah
Ezekiel
Daniel
Hosea
Joel, Amos, and Obadiah
Jonah, Micah, and Nahum
Haggai, Zechariah, and Malachi
Matthew
Mark
Luke
John

Acts
Romans
1 Corinthians
2 Corinthians
Galatians
Ephesians
Philippians
Colossians and Philemon
1–2 Thessalonians
1–2 Timothy and Titus
Hebrews
James
1–2 Peter and Jude
1–3 John
Revelation

The Ten Commandments   The Sermon on the Mount   The Parables of Jesus

• • • • • •

DOUGLAS SEAN O'DONNELL (PhD, University of Aberdeen) is the Senior Vice President of Bible Editorial at Crossway. He is the author and editor of more than a dozen books, including *The Beginning and End of Wisdom*; *The Pastor's Book*; *The Song of Solomon* and *Matthew* in the Preaching the Word commentary series; and *Psalms* and *The Parables of Jesus* in the *Knowing the Bible* series. He also contributed "Song of Solomon" and "Job" to the ESV Expository Commentary.

THE PARABLES OF JESUS

A 12-WEEK STUDY

Douglas Sean O'Donnell

WHEATON, ILLINOIS

Knowing the Bible: The Parables of Jesus, A 12-Week Study

Copyright © 2023 by Crossway

Published by Crossway
    1300 Crescent Street
    Wheaton, Illinois 60187

Cover design: Simplicated Studio

First printing 2023

Printed in the United States of America

Trade paperback ISBN: 978-1-4335-8944-7

EPub ISBN: 978-1-4335-8947-8
PDF ISBN: 978-1-4335-8945-4

Crossway is a publishing ministry of Good News Publishers.

VP			33	32	31	30	29	28	27	26	25	24	23
15	14	13	12	11	10	9	8	7	6	5	4	3	2	1

TABLE OF CONTENTS

▲

SERIES PREFACE

KNOWING THE BIBLE, as the title indicates, was created to help readers know and understand the meaning, the message, and the God of the Bible. This series was created and edited by Lane Dennis and Dane Ortlund, and J. I. Packer served as the theological editor. Dr. Packer has gone to be with the Lord, Lane has retired as CEO and president of Crossway, and Dane now serves as senior pastor of Naperville (Illinois) Presbyterian Church. We are so grateful for their labors in overseeing the first forty-plus volumes of this series! To honor and expand upon their idea, we are continuing the series, focusing on key sections from Scripture, such as the Ten Commandments and the Sermon on the Mount.

Each volume in the series consists of twelve units that progressively take the reader through a clear, concise, and deep study of certain portions of Scripture. The material works best for a small group, as the questions are designed for good interactive group discussion. Even so, an individual could easily use the material for a personal Bible study as well.

Week 1 provides an overview of the section or sections of Scripture to be studied, which includes placing the text into its larger context (e.g., the Sermon on the Mount within the Gospel of Matthew), providing key historical background, and offering some questions to get started. Weeks 2–12 each have the following features: a summary of how the text fits into the rest of Scripture ("The Place of the Passage"), a summary sentence on the main theme ("The Big Picture"), and ten or so questions ("Reflection and Discussion Questions"). Moreover, each unit highlights the role of the gospel of grace in each text ("Gospel Glimpses"), identifies whole-Bible themes ("Whole-Bible Connections"), pinpoints Christian doctrines ("Theological Soundings"), defines key terms ("Definitions"), and allows space to respond ("Personal Implications").

Lastly, to help readers understand the Bible better, we urge readers to use the ESV Bible and the *ESV Study Bible*, which are available in various print and digital formats, including online editions at esv.org. The *Knowing the Bible* series is also available online.

May our gracious God, who has generously given his Spirit and his Word, use this study to grow his people in their knowledge and love of the Father, Son, and Spirit.

Douglas Sean O'Donnell
Series Editor

Week 1: Overview

Getting Acquainted

If you are familiar with the Gospels, you know that parables play a prominent part in Jesus' teaching. Depending on how one defines the Greek term *parabolē*,[1] which occurs fifty-two times in the New Testament (mostly in Matthew and Luke), the Gospels record up to seventy parables, including forty narrative ones.[2] This study will focus on some of the most famous narrative parables, such as the parables of the sower and the seed, the good Samaritan, the rich fool, and the prodigal son. This study will also feature a variety of different types of parables, such as parables of judgment, extended comparisons, and example stories.

Most of us enjoy reading and hearing Jesus' parables. However, we often struggle as much as his first disciples, who asked "what" a particular "parable meant" (Luke 8:9). And just as those first disciples asked Jesus how to pray ("Lord, teach us to pray," 11:1), so we need his help in understanding the "secrets of the kingdom of God" revealed in the parables (8:10). We trust that this Bible study will prove invaluable in your quest for such knowledge through the eye-opening work of the Holy Spirit.

Placing Them in the Larger Story

Jesus' parables are not merely simple, short narratives that teach morals. They are similes and stories that help us understand the nature of the kingdom of God and point us to the King of that kingdom. Thus, when we study the individual parables, we must think about how the parables relate to how Jesus fulfills the promises of the Hebrew Scriptures (Old Testament) and how he embodies various characters in his stories—the heaven-sent Son, the bridegroom, the king upon his glorious throne, the judge on judgment day.

Key Verse

When his disciples asked [Jesus] what this parable meant, he said, "To you it has been given to know the secrets of the kingdom of God, but for others they are in parables, so that 'seeing they may not see, and hearing they may not understand'" (Luke 8:9–10).

Date and Historical Background

Mark (the earliest Gospel) was written in perhaps the mid- to late-50s AD, roughly twenty-five years after the death and resurrection of Jesus. Mark contains only two narrative parables (found also in Matthew and Luke), while Matthew contains ten unique parables and Luke fifteen. Jesus' parables have appealed to billions of people living over two millennia. Yet it is important to understand them first as set within their original context (first-century Palestine) and audience (mostly Jews). How would the original audience have understood the parables? And, since Christ's parables were intentionally provocative, what would have shocked his first hearers? For example, a Samaritan as the hero in a story about loving others would have shocked Jewish cultural and spiritual sensibilities.

As You Get Started

As stated above, Jesus preached around forty narrative parables.[2] There is some precedent in the Old Testament for Jesus' teaching style. Read Judges 9:7–15; 2 Samuel 12:1–4; 2 Kings 14:9–10; Ezekiel 17:2–10; and Isaiah 5:1–7. How do these forms and stories resemble what you know of Christ's parables?

Why did Jesus teach in parables? This question will be answered by Jesus in the next study. But, without turning there for the answer, give your best answer now.

_____

_____

_____

_____

_____

_____

_____

What does Mark mean when he writes that Christ Jesus "did not speak to them without a parable" (Mark 4:34)? Let these next three questions help you find the answer. First, to whom does the pronoun "them" refer in the immediate context? How many full-scale narrative parables are recorded in Mark's Gospel? And, would you categorize the following statements as parables: "The time is fulfilled, and the kingdom of God is at hand; repent and believe in the gospel" (1:15)? "Follow me, and I will make you become fishers of men" (1:17)? "Son, your sins are forgiven" (2:5)?

_____

_____

_____

_____

_____

_____

_____

_____

What are you looking forward to in your study of the parables?

_____

_____

_____

_____

_____

_____

_____

Jesus begins the parable of the sower with this exhortation: "Listen! Behold, a sower went out to sow" (Mark 4:3). A dozen times Jesus calls his listeners to "hear" (e.g., "Hear another parable"; Matt. 21:33) and twice to "hear . . . and understand" (15:10; Mark 7:14). How do Jesus' calls to listen help us know how to pray as we begin this study?

As You Finish This Unit . . .

Take a moment now to ask for the Lord's blessing and help as you engage in this study of Jesus' parables. And take a moment also to look back through this unit of study, to reflect on a few key things that the Lord may be teaching you—and perhaps to highlight or underline these to review again in the future.

Definitions

[1] **Parable** – Robert Kinney offers this definition: "A parable is a simple and usually narrative story, grounded in the real world, and used to provoke the audience on a spiritual (or moral) matter or even to make a spiritual (or moral) point." The word itself is a combination of the Greek preposition *para* ("beside") and the verb *ballō* ("to cast"), thus literally meaning to "toss next to" or "to place alongside." A parable makes a comparison: God is like the longing and loving father who forgives and embraces a prodigal son who returns home; the growth of the kingdom of God is like the growth of a mustard seed. The two compared realities are alike in some way, and together they teach theological truths and spiritual lessons.

[2] **Narrative parables** – Symbolic stories that are one type of parable used by Christ. Jesus taught with three types of parables. First are his aphorisms ("Can a blind man lead a blind man? Will they not both fall into a pit?" Luke 6:39). Second are similes ("The kingdom of heaven is like treasure hidden in a field"; Matt. 13:44). Third are symbolic stories (the parable of the sower), also called narrative parables.

WEEK 2: THE SOWER

Mark 4:1–20

▲

The Place of the Passage

Jesus' parable of the sower is found in Matthew (13:1–23), Mark (4:1–20), and Luke (8:4–15). In Mark's Gospel the parable is told during Jesus' later Galilean ministry (Mark 3:13–6:6), alongside the only concentrated section on parables in the whole Gospel. Both this parable and the others in Mark 4 help to explain what the kingdom of God[1] is like.

The Big Picture

This parable is told both to encourage Jesus' disciples (that people will receive "the word," Mark 4:14; that is, "the word of God,"[2] 7:13) and to inform them to expect opposition and rejection to the gospel of the kingdom.

> ## Reflection and Discussion

Read through the complete passage for this study, Mark 4:1–20. Then think through and write your own notes on the following questions. (See *ESV Study Bible* notes on pages 1899–1900; online at www.esv.org.)

As Jesus "began to teach" beside the Sea of Galilee (Mark 4:1), why might "a very large crowd" have gathered? What has Jesus said and done in the first three chapters to draw such attention?

Most people in the crowd, even those who were not farmers, would be familiar with sowing seed. How would these first hearers have understood the parable? What do you suppose they thought Jesus was teaching in this parable?

Mark records that Jesus "was teaching [the crowd] in parables" (Mark 4:2) and later that Jesus "did not speak" to the crowd on that day "without a parable" (v. 34). According to Jesus in Mark 4:10–12, why does he teach in parables? See also verses 33–34 and especially Matthew 13:11–17.

In Mark 4:12, Jesus offers a condensed quote of Isaiah 6:9–10. Turn to Isaiah and read the quote in full. Then skim through Isaiah 1–5 and answer two questions. First, what are God's people in Isaiah's time doing that is upsetting God? Second, how is Jesus' preaching in parables similar to Isaiah's ministry?

In the Gospel of Mark, how has Jesus and his message been received thus far? How does such reception shed light on the themes found in the parable of the sower?

For most parables Jesus does not reveal their symbolism, or second level of meaning. But in Mark 4:14–20 he does so for everything except "the sower." Fill in the chart below, including who you think the sower is and what "the word" (in the context of Mark and the New Testament) is.

Detail	Referent
Sower	
Seed	The word
Path	
Birds	
Rocky ground	
Thorn-infested soil	
Good soil	

How does Jesus' explanation above help us interpret the parables he does not explain?

_____

_____

_____

_____

_____

Write down at least one lesson we can learn from each key detail. For example, we might say that, just as the sower sowed seed, we should share the gospel, knowing that God promises remarkable growth despite many possible hindrances.

Seed	
Path	
Birds	
Rocky ground	
Thorn-infested soil	
Good soil	

How do the parables of the growing seed (4:26–29) and the mustard seed (4:30–32) expand upon the theme of positive reception of the word (the good soil)?

_____

_____

_____

_____

_____

What is the central application of the parable of the sower?

_____

_____

_____

_____

_____

When was the last time you shared the gospel with a nonbeliever? What was the response? How should this parable give you confidence to share the gospel in the future?

Read through the following three sections on *Gospel Glimpses, Whole-Bible Connections*, and *Theological Soundings*. Then take time to consider the *Personal Implications* these sections have for you.

Gospel Glimpses

GOSPEL GROWTH. When Jesus speaks of the grain in the good soil "yielding thirtyfold and sixtyfold and a hundredfold" (Mark 4:8; compare v. 20), he is describing an overabundant harvest. In ancient Israel it was difficult to produce consistently good harvests. If a farmer got sevenfold what he planted, he would be satisfied. To produce tenfold would be considered a good harvest, and twentyfold an excellent harvest; to receive thirtyfold, sixtyfold, or a hundredfold would be an unfathomable yield. With this amazing harvest in mind, Jesus ends his parable on a very positive note. Those who abide in him and his word bear fruit. Some a lot of fruit. Others even more than a lot. Still others many bushelsful.

BLESSED EYES. To the self-righteous and those who have met Jesus' ministry with indifference (Matt. 11:20), misunderstanding (12:46), unbelief (13:58), or hostile opposition (12:10, 14, 24), "the secrets of the kingdom of heaven" (13:11) remain hidden. Jesus' parables serve, in some way, as divine judgments. For the disciples, however, parables serve a different purpose. Parables do not conceal the truth but reveal it. They are expressions of God's gracious mercy. To those who persist in unbelief, the mystery of the gospel of the kingdom is not seen, but, to those receptive to what God is doing in Jesus, parables are like looking at stained-glass windows from the inside while the sun pours through. For the twelve, Jesus affirms their unique spiritual privilege: "Blessed are your eyes, for they see, and your ears, for they hear" (13:16). They have been chosen to be scribes "trained" by Jesus to grasp and give to others the "treasure" of "the kingdom of heaven" (13:52).

Whole-Bible Connections

SEEING BUT NOT SEEING. In Isaiah 6:9–10 God warned the prophet that many would grasp the content of his message yet reject its truth. In Mark 4:12 (and parallels in Matt. 13:13–15; Luke 8:10) Jesus cites Isaiah to show that his parables have a similar function. They are simple stories full of everyday images, yet they require us to admit that we—like Isaiah's audience (see Isaiah 1–4)—are rebels in need of God's forgiveness. To embrace genuinely such truth requires insight that only God's Spirit can give (1 Cor. 2:12–14).

THE MYSTERY OF THE KINGDOM. Jesus launched his ministry with the startling announcement that "the kingdom of God is at hand" (Mark 1:15; Matt. 4:17). Yet the kingdom's arrival did not match people's expectations. Two things were expected to occur immediately and simultaneously: God would save his people and judge his enemies. But Mark 4 tells us that the kingdom of heaven has indeed arrived in Jesus, but it will not be fully consummated until the distant future. Like a tiny mustard seed that grows into a tree, the kingdom begins small and grows into its full expression over time (4:31–32).

Theological Soundings

TRUE AND FALSE FAITH. Jesus' parable of the sower shows four different responses to his message. The first one "hears the word of the kingdom" but "does not understand it" (Matt. 13:19; compare Mark 4:15). The second responds joyfully but then falls away[3] (Mark 4:16–17). The third endures for a while but "proves unfruitful" (v. 19). Only the fourth proves to be fruitful (v. 20). What might appear on the surface to be faith may prove to be false. Only the fourth kind of hearers are genuine, as evidenced by their fruitfulness. As Jesus says, "The tree is known by its fruit" (Matt. 12:33–35; see 7:15–20).

SATAN. From the first pages of Genesis, human sin is presented as a betrayal of God by means of man's placing his trust in the lies of Satan instead of trusting God's word. In our modern secular age, Christians are eager to defend the reality of a good God, but we often neglect the reality of "the evil one" (Matt. 13:19), who seeks to "steal and kill and destroy" (John 10:10). In this parable, Satan destroys by coming and stealing away the word that is sown (Matt. 13:19) in people who initially receive the gospel.

GOD'S SOVEREIGNTY AND HUMAN RESPONSIBILITY. Jesus repeatedly teaches that God is ultimately sovereign over the ability of people to understand his revelation. The ability to "hear" spiritually the message of the kingdom is a gift that God gives only to some (Matt. 13:10–11). At the same time, he calls *all* to "hear" his message (v. 18; similarly, see 11:25–27). Throughout the Bible we see that God is sovereign over all things but that humans are nonetheless responsible for their actions. The reality of both truths together in Scripture means that we must not reject one to preserve the other. God is sovereign, and humans are responsible. As difficult as it may be for us to hold these twin truths together, they are ultimately compatible, not contradictory.

Personal Implications

Take time to reflect on the implications of Mark 4:1–20 for your own life today. Consider what you have learned that might lead you to praise God, repent of sin, and trust in his gracious promises. Make notes below on the *Personal Implications* for your walk with the Lord of the (1) *Gospel Glimpses*, (2) *Whole-Bible Connections*, (3) *Theological Soundings*, and (4) the passage as a whole.

1. Gospel Glimpses

2. Whole-Bible Connections

3. Theological Soundings

4. Mark 4:1–20

> ### As You Finish This Unit . . .

Take a moment now to ask for the Lord's blessing and help as you continue in this study of Jesus' parables. And take a moment also to look back through this unit of study, to reflect on a few key things that the Lord may be teaching you—and perhaps to highlight or underline these to review again in the future.

Definitions

[1] **Kingdom of God** – The rule of God manifested in the long-awaited restoration of his people and indeed the whole world, in which God will reign over the glad submission of all people.

[2] **The word of God** – In Mark, the message of the gospel (note 1:1, 14–15) or the saving news of what God is doing in Jesus to restore the world. The word of God, we learn in Mark 4, is powerful and fruitful, yet also dividing and alienating.

[3] **Falling away** – A metaphorical way of describing either a temporary renunciation ("You will all fall away"; Mark 14:27) or a permanent apostasy (see Hebrews 6) that leads to eternal judgment (3:12; 12:15). Only Jesus can keep believers from falling away (see Luke 22:31; John 16:1).

WEEK 3: THE GOOD SAMARITAN

Luke 10:25–37

▲

The Place of the Passage

While the Gospel of John contains extended metaphors (e.g., John 10:1–18; 15:1–8), it contains no parables. The Synoptic Gospels[1] (mostly Matthew and Luke), however, record up to seventy parables. Nine of those parables are found in both Matthew and Luke. Matthew provides ten unique parables, and Luke sixteen. The parable of the good Samaritan is one of those parables unique to Luke. It comes near the start of what is known as Luke's travel narrative (Luke 9:51–19:27), in which Jesus "set his face to go to Jerusalem" (9:51).

The Big Picture

As Jesus journeys toward the cross, he challenges his followers to do two things: reorient their vision of God and his character and priorities; and live in a way that reflects this new vision. The parable of the good Samaritan fits in perfectly with those goals.

Reflection and Discussion

Read through the complete passage for this study, Luke 10:25–37. Then think through and write your own notes on the following questions. (See *ESV Study Bible* notes on pages 1976–1977; online at www.esv.org.)

Think of a time when you saw someone in need—perhaps a homeless man asking for food or a family with car trouble at the side of the road. Did you stop to help? If not, why? Were you busy or running late? Was it inconvenient? Were you afraid?

Does the man who approaches Jesus and asks him a question approach him with pure motives? Why does Jesus answer the man's question with a question of his own?

What is good about this man's question (10:25)? What is not so good? (For help with your answer, turn to Luke 10:21–24 and read what Jesus teaches right before this passage.)

A "lawyer," in Jesus' day, was a scholar who was an expert in the law of Moses.[2] This is why the lawyer quotes from Deuteronomy 6:4–5 and Leviticus 19:18.

Jesus applauds his answer: "You have answered correctly; do this, and you will live" (Luke 10:28). Since we know from elsewhere in Scripture (e.g., Rom. 3:20) that no one can keep the law perfectly, why do you think Jesus says this?

In Luke 10:29, Luke offers an insight into the lawyer's internal thoughts: "He, desiring to justify himself, said to Jesus, 'And who is my neighbor?'" The lawyer is wanting to limit whom he has to love. Why, then, is Jesus' parable an ingenious answer to his question?

Both the priest[3] and the Levite are journeying from Jerusalem, where they have presumably led God's people in worship through sacrifices (e.g., Lev. 4:26) and songs (e.g., 1 Chron. 15:22). How do their religious callings heighten the hypocrisy of their actions? What is one way you could apply what Jesus implies here?

A priest was commanded not to touch a dead body, for in doing so he would "make himself unclean" (see Lev. 21:1). Look carefully at Luke 10:30. Could this priest use that excuse? Moreover, how do the principles Jesus teaches in Matthew 12:11; 23:23 apply here?

Thanks to this parable, in the Western world the word *Samaritan*[4] has good connotations. For example, many hospitals are called Good Samaritan Hospital, and most states have what are called "good Samaritan laws," which legally protect people who attempt to aid victims and in doing so inadvertently harm the person. To a Jew of Jesus' day, however, what was so shocking about Jesus' making the hero a Samaritan (see Luke 9:52–54; John 4:9, 27; 8:48)? What might be an equivalent today?

List all the characters in the parable. Who are the main ones? Often Jesus has a lesson to teach based on how each main character thinks, speaks, and acts. What is the point of application for each character?

When Augustine interpreted this parable, he claimed that Jerusalem was the heavenly city; that the man who was mugged was Adam (who fell into sin, just as this man fell into the hands of the robbers); that the priest and Levite represent the Law and the Prophets (neither of which saves); and that the inn is the church (where the oil of baptism and the wine of communion are administered). Do you think it is appropriate to symbolize each character and detail in this way? Why or why not?

What is certainly appropriate to say is that the mercy of the Samaritan symbolizes the greater mercy of Jesus Christ. Jesus goes out of his way to save us when we are not merely injured but dead because of our sin. What are some other connections to Christ here?

Read through the following three sections on *Gospel Glimpses, Whole-Bible Connections*, and *Theological Soundings*. Then take time to consider the *Personal Implications* these sections have for you.

Gospel Glimpses

LOVE AS THE FRUIT OF LOVE. Some have understood the parable of the good Samaritan to teach salvation by works: if we love our needy neighbors, we will "inherit eternal life" (Luke 10:25). In fact, however, three features of the parable demonstrate our need for the *gift* of salvation. (1) Without a deep heart change, even knowing our duty will not motivate us to do it (v. 29). (2) Jesus calls for the kind of love that counts even an enemy as a neighbor, a mark of those transformed by God's mercy (6:27–36). (3) Jesus speaks this parable as he journeys toward Jerusalem (9:51) to secure eternal life for us. Strength to love our neighbors is the fruit of the love God shows us in his Son.

THE COMPASSION AND MERCY OF THE LORD. In James 5:11, Jesus' brother reminds us of how the Lord is compassionate and merciful. Those truths lie at the very heart of the good news of Christianity. It is God's love for sinners—his loving attitude (compassion) and actions (mercy)—that leads him to save us. As Paul writes, "God shows his love for us in that while we were still sinners, Christ died for us" (Rom. 5:8).

Whole-Bible Connections

THE TWO GREATEST COMMANDMENTS. Jesus teaches that all of God's law is summarized in the commandments to love God and neighbor (Matt. 22:37–40; Mark 12:29–31; Luke 10:27). The fact that both of these commandments are found in the law of Moses (Deut. 6:4–5; Lev. 19:18) and are detailed in the Ten Commandments (first four commandments, our relationship with God; last six, our relationships with neighbors) demonstrates the unity of Scripture and shows that Jesus knows Scripture and knows how to explain it. The New Testament certainly reveals new depths and dimensions of love (see John 13:34–35; 1 John 4:7–11, 19), but love for God and neighbor has always been at the heart of Scripture.

SAMARITANS AND THE SPIRIT. The Samaritans were considered racial "half-breeds." As we see in the Gospels, even Jesus' first Jewish disciples had difficulty when Samaritans received the blessings of Jesus the Messiah. In Acts this issue of acceptance resurfaces. Jesus' mission is clear: the twelve, after they receive power when the Holy Spirit comes upon them, are to be Jesus' "witnesses in Jerusalem and in all Judea [to Jews] and Samaria [to Samaritans], and to the end of the earth [to all the Gentile nations]" (Acts 1:8). But it is not until God bestows the gift of the Holy Spirit (8:17) on those Samaritans who "had received the word of God" (v. 14) that both Jewish and Samaritan Christians understand that they are united spiritually and are members of the same body of Christ.

Theological Soundings

THE MOTIVATION FOR MISSION. The word Matthew, Mark, and Luke use most often to describe Jesus' emotional response to physical and spiritual needs is "compassion." For example, in both of Jesus' miraculous feedings, before he feeds the crowd he has "compassion" on them (Matt. 14:14; 15:32). Jesus' compassion compels him to send the disciples on their mission. Jesus' compassionate heart still drives the church's mission today.

THE SCOPE OF THE CHURCH'S MISSION. From Genesis 1:1 through Revelation 22:21, God reveals himself as a missionary God. Through Abraham (Gen. 12:1–3) God promises to bless all the nations of the earth, and that promise finds its fulfillment in Jesus Christ. He is the promised descendant of Abraham—the true and final offspring (Gal. 3:16)—who receives the inheritance and shares it with all who are united to him by faith, regardless of their ethnicity (Gal. 3:6–29). Through Christ's redeemed people, God will take the gospel to all nations (Matt. 28:18–20).

Personal Implications

Take time to reflect on the implications of Luke 10:25–37 for your own life today. Consider what you have learned that might lead you to praise God, repent of sin,

and trust in his gracious promises. Make notes below on the *Personal Implications* for your walk with the Lord of the (1) *Gospel Glimpses*, (2) *Whole-Bible Connections*, (3) *Theological Soundings*, and (4) the passage as a whole.

1. Gospel Glimpses

2. Whole-Bible Connections

3. Theological Soundings

4. Luke 10:25–37

As You Finish This Unit . . .

Take a moment now to ask for the Lord's blessing and help as you continue in this study of Jesus' parables. And take a moment also to look back through this unit of study, to reflect on a few key things that the Lord may be teaching you—and perhaps to highlight or underline these to review again in the future.

Definitions

[1] **Synoptic Gospels** – The Gospels of Matthew, Mark, and Luke. They are labeled "synoptic" (from roots meaning "to see together") because they include a number of the same narratives and teachings of Jesus.

[2] **Law of Moses** – The first five books of the Bible, also called the Pentateuch or the Torah.

[3] **Priest** – In Old Testament Israel the priest represented the people before God and represented God before the people. Although the whole tribe of Levites was given duties overseeing worship, only those descended from Aaron could be priests. Prescribed duties of priests also included inspecting and receiving sacrifices from the people and overseeing the daily activities and maintenance of the temple.

[4] **Samaritan** – A person from Samaria, which was populated with people who were part Jew and part Gentile.

WEEK 4: THE RICH FOOL

Luke 12:13–21

▲

The Place of the Passage

Luke 13:22 reminds us that Jesus is still "journeying toward Jerusalem" and therefore toward his death and resurrection. From this point through 17:11 (where we read a third and final description of Jesus' progress toward Jerusalem) Jesus continues to reshape our vision of God and of a God-honoring life. He does so by calling his hearers to embrace the "inside-out" priorities of God's kingdom, to commit to the radical demands of discipleship, and to repent, especially of an idolatrous love of wealth.

The Big Picture

Throughout the Gospel of Luke Jesus warns about the dangers of wealth, perhaps no more strongly and surprisingly than in his parable of the rich fool.

Reflection and Discussion

Read through the complete passage for this study, Luke 12:13–21. Then think through and write your own notes on the following questions. (See *ESV Study Bible* notes on page 1982; online at www.esv.org.)

When your parents or oldest living relatives die, who in your family will receive the inheritance? How might our practice today differ from the typical inheritance laws[1] of Jesus' day?

Review what happens before the parable, in Luke 12:13–15. Does "someone" from "the crowd" ask Jesus a question, as most people who approach Jesus do, or does that person command Jesus to act?

In Jesus' second response to the man (Luke 12:15), what does he detect to be this man's root sin? Turn to Exodus 20:17. How does the Bible define this sin? Of the three parts of the tenth commandment—related to one's neighbor's house, spouse, and workforce—with which part do you struggle the most?

When Jesus offers the reason why one should not covet ("one's life does not consist in the abundance of his possessions"; Luke 12:15), he reminds us that "the abundance of . . . possessions" is not essential to our *survival* (we can live without a lot!); it does not necessarily lead to *happiness* (often the opposite); and it offers *no protection* against sickness, sorrows, calamities, or death. That said, why do we find Jesus' teaching here so hard to believe?

How many times does the rich man speak about himself—using the words "I," "he," "himself," and "my"? What is Jesus emphasizing?

In Deuteronomy 8:18 Moses admonishes, "You shall remember the LORD your God, for it is *he who gives you power to get wealth.*" Do you think that way about your wealth? Why or why not? Does the rich man thank God for his success? Read Romans 1:18–21. According to Paul, how serious is the sin of ingratitude?

This rich man expresses no thought of God. Nor does he express any thought *of others* or offer any help *to others*. Instead, his focus is on himself. "Soul," he says to himself, "you have ample goods laid up for many years; relax, eat, drink, be merry" (Luke 12:19). Read Luke 12:32–34; 18:22. What does Jesus think about such behavior?

Read Acts 2:45. Have you ever sold any of your possessions and given the money from the sale directly to someone in need? How would such a regular practice offer an antidote to coveting, which Paul labels "idolatry"[2] (Col. 3:5)?

How is the rich man presumptuous? What has he not taken into account? How is his attitude different from what is taught in James 4:13–16?

In Deuteronomy 8, Moses offers a warning regarding the time when God will bring Israel "into a good land," a land in which they "will eat bread without scarcity" and will "be full" (Deut. 8:7–10). What key word is repeated most in the verses that follow (vv. 11–19)? Why?

As Jesus concludes his thought-provoking parable, he issues a final admonition: "So is the one who lays up treasure for himself and is not rich toward God" (Luke 12:21). If the main application of the parable of the rich fool is to be "rich toward God" (v. 21), what does that look like? Answers are provided in the immediate context—Jesus' teaching in verses 22–34. How do we apply these answers?

Read through the following three sections on *Gospel Glimpses, Whole-Bible Connections*, and *Theological Soundings*. Then take time to consider the *Personal Implications* these sections have for you.

Gospel Glimpses

JESUS BECAME POOR. In one of the most remarkable statements about Jesus in the Bible Paul writes, "You know the grace of our Lord Jesus Christ, that though he was rich, yet for your sake he became poor, so that you by his poverty might become rich" (2 Cor. 8:9). Jesus' *poverty* was his incarnation. The eternal and ever-glorious Son of God was born of a woman who was not wealthy, and he was raised in a small and obscure village. More than that, he lived a humble life of dependence on both his heavenly Father and his earthly friends and followers. Then, through his sacrificial sufferings and death, he gave everything away. Such sacrifice (his extreme poverty!) bestows the riches of God's salvation upon all who trust in him.

LIGHT OF THE WORLD. After the parable of the rich fool, Jesus teaches that one of the ways in which we can be "rich toward God" (Luke 12:21) includes seeking his kingdom (v. 31), or the spread of the reign of Christ on earth, and that one of the ways in which we can do this is by sharing our God-given provisions with others: "Sell your possessions, and give to the needy" (v. 33). Neither here nor anywhere else in the New Testament are Christians instructed (as some have claimed) to "preach the gospel at all times, and use words if necessary." Words are always necessary! The gospel cannot be preached without the proclamation of who Jesus is and what he has done. That said, both here in Luke 12 and elsewhere it is clear that declaration and demonstration of the gospel go hand in hand (see Matt 5:1–16; 1 Peter 2:9–12; 3:1). People are often won to Christ when our works match our words.

Whole-Bible Connections

DECEITFULNESS OF RICHES. Back in the garden, Adam and Eve had everything they needed but were cast out because they chose to eat from the one tree that was off-limits. From that point on, the desire for more has plagued God's people. Throughout Israel's history, the test set before God's people was whether they would be content with the good gifts and boundaries given by God, or would seek fulfillment elsewhere. In the New Testament, Jesus warns about the deceitfulness of riches (Matt. 6:24; 13:22) and the futility of greed (19:22–24; Luke 12:16–20). Moreover, he admonishes us to be "rich toward God" (Luke 12:21), to seek first his kingdom (12:31), and to trust and thank God for his provision (Matt. 6:19–33). Following Jesus (1 Tim. 6:3), Paul speaks of the damnable dangers of the love of money (v. 10) and of the uncertainty of riches, and he charges wealthy Christians to "set their hopes . . . on God, who richly provides us with everything to enjoy" (v. 17).

THE SON OF MAN. In Psalm 8:4, "son of man" is a designation for humanity as a whole, given dominion over the earth at creation. In Daniel 7:13–14 the "son of man" is a glorious figure to whom God gives an "everlasting dominion" and who (like God) is to be honored and served by "all peoples." Jesus' use of the title (his favorite self-designation) is therefore a claim to be a divine-human mediator who exercises dominion faithfully over all things—even death (Heb. 2:6–9). The Son of Man exercises this dominion through his suffering (Luke 17:25; 18:31–33), his exaltation (Acts 7:56; Rev. 1:13), and his future return to judge the earth (Luke 17:24, 30; 18:8; Rev. 14:14).

Theological Soundings

JESUS THE JUDGE. Jesus' question "Man, who made me a judge or arbitrator over you?" (see Luke 12:14) is dripping with irony,[3] for we know that one day this man and all people "must all appear before the judgment seat of Christ" (2 Cor. 5:10), which is also called the "great white throne" (Rev. 20:11). In fact, Jesus teaches in Matthew 25:31–32 that "when the Son of Man comes in glory . . . then he will sit on his glorious throne," and "before him will be gathered all the nations" to be judged. Some will receive the sentence of "eternal punishment" and others the reward of "eternal life" (25:46); some will hear, "Depart from me, you cursed, into the eternal fire prepared for the devil and his angels" (25:41: compare 7:23), while others will hear, "Come, you who are blessed by my Father, inherit the kingdom prepared for you from the foundation of the world" (v. 34), along with the words "Well done, good and faithful servant. . . . Enter into the joy of your master" (v. 21).

LOVE OF MONEY. Money promises security and pleasure, but those who love money will never have enough to be satisfied (Eccles. 5:10). Jesus teaches plainly, "You cannot serve God and money" (Luke 16:13). Moreover, as Paul teaches, riches are fleeting and uncertain (1 Tim. 6:7, 17), and clamoring after them will bring not satisfaction but sorrow and ultimate "ruin and destruction" (vv. 9–10). The solution, however, is not asceticism or vows of poverty. Rather, we should be content with what we have and should bank our hopes on God, who will abundantly provide (vv. 8, 17). All of God's people—especially the rich—must recognize God as the giver of all good things (James 1:17). They must use their God-given financial means to be generous to others and thus "store up treasure" for the life to come (1 Tim. 6:19; Matt. 6:20).

> **Personal Implications**

Take time to reflect on the implications of Luke 12:13–21 for your own life today. Consider what you have learned that might lead you to praise God, repent of sin, and trust in his gracious promises. Make notes below on the *Personal Implications* for your walk with the Lord of the (1) *Gospel Glimpses*, (2) *Whole-Bible Connections*, (3) *Theological Soundings*, and (4) the passage as a whole.

1. Gospel Glimpses

2. Whole-Bible Connections

3. Theological Soundings

4. Luke 12:13–21

As You Finish This Unit . . .

Take a moment now to ask for the Lord's blessing and help as you continue in this study of Jesus' parables. And take a moment also to look back through this unit of study, to reflect on a few key things that the Lord may be teaching you—and perhaps to highlight or underline these to review again in the future.

Definitions

[1] **Inheritance laws** – In Jesus' day, typically the oldest son would receive his father's land and twice the inheritance that his younger brother(s) would receive. This was because he was to provide for his father's household, which might include his father's widow, other children (unmarried daughters), servants, and animals.

[2] **Idolatry** – In the Bible, idolatry usually refers to the worship of a physical object. Paul's comments in Colossians 3:5, however, indicate that idolatry can include covetousness, which is essentially equivalent to worshiping material things.

[3] **Irony** – A literary device by which an author, for rhetorical effect, expresses something using language that normally signifies the opposite of his intended meaning.

WEEK 5: THE PRODIGAL SON

Luke 15:11–32

The Place of the Passage

Like the parable of the rich fool, the parable of the prodigal[1] son is found within the narratives that record Jesus' journey "toward Jerusalem" (Luke 13:22). At every step closer to the cross, Jesus teaches about the countercultural characteristics and commitments of God's kingdom. As he does so, opposition to his pronouncements and predictions mount, especially from the Jewish religious leaders and eventually the Roman authorities.

The Big Picture

The parable of the prodigal son is a word picture of Jesus' mission of reception and fellowship with repentant sinners.

> ### Reflection and Discussion

Read through the complete passage for this study, Luke 15:11–32. Then think through and write your own notes on the following questions. (See *ESV Study Bible* notes on pages 1989–1990; online at www.esv.org.)

Before turning to the parable of the prodigal son, look at the preceding context. How would you summarize the shared themes in the three parables of Luke 15? Look for key repeated words.

What circumstances lead to Jesus' telling of these three parables, and how do they offer a defense of Jesus' actions of receiving and relating with tax collectors[2] and sinners (Luke 15:1–2)?

How does what is said in Luke 16:14 shed further light on the Jewish religious leaders? How about Jesus' parable of the dishonest manager (vv. 1–9) and his teaching regarding money (vv. 10–13)?

Look at Luke 15:11–16. A story, no matter how short, involves setting, characters, and plot. Where are the two places (one assumed, the other named) that constitute the setting? Who are the characters? What is the problem presented at the beginning of the story?

What do the father's actions teach us about him? Do you think he is gullible? Generous? An optimist?

Read Luke 15:17. How important is it that we come to the end of ourselves, or hit rock bottom ("he came to himself"), before we come to recognize our need for grace and redemption? Do you have a story like that? If so, are you willing to share it with the group?

In the younger brother's coming-back-to-his-senses speech to himself, how many times does he use the word "Father," and why might this repetition be significant?

How much of his rehearsed repentance[3] is the son able to blurt out before his father stops him? While the father says nothing to the son (which is interesting!),

what does he say to his servants that shows his love and forgiveness[4] of his son?
What does this part of the story (Luke 15:20–24) teach us about God the Father?

In Luke 15:25–32 the older brother takes center stage. We have learned lessons
from the father and younger brother. What lesson, or lessons, do we learn from
the older brother's reaction to his brother's repentance and his father's forgiveness? Moreover, and to return full circle, how might the older brother's reaction
relate to what is recorded in 15:1–2?

We do not read of the older brother's response to his father. Why might Jesus
end the parable in this inconclusive way?

Read through the following three sections on *Gospel Glimpses, Whole-Bible Connections*, and *Theological Soundings*. Then take time to consider the *Personal
Implications* these sections have for you.

Gospel Glimpses

THE PRODIGAL FATHER. The real scandal of the parable of the prodigal son
(Luke 15:11–32) is the excess with which the father, representing God, lavishes

love on his younger son. According to Jesus, the God of heaven delights to run to us (v. 20), to bestow on us the status of sons and daughters (v. 22), and to compromise his own dignity in order to enhance ours. In Jesus, this God endures not only angry criticism (see vv. 2, 28–30) but torment and death—all in order to shower love on anyone who will repent and rest in his mercy.

JESUS RECEIVES SINNERS. The word "sinners" in Luke 15:1 does not mean regular sinful humans ("we are all sinners"; see Rom. 3:23). Rather, it implies a criminal class of people, usually Jews who made a living through lawless living. The term here is often paired with "tax collectors" or "prostitutes" in the Synoptics (Matt. 21:31, 32). Yet it is "the tax collectors and sinners" who "were all drawing near" to listen to Jesus (Luke 15:1). Elsewhere in Luke, Jesus calls a "tax collector named Levi" (5:27) to follow him, and Levi accepts the call. We also know that, soon after, Jesus dines in Levi's house with a "large company of tax collectors" (v. 29). Jesus' fellowship with such notorious sinners is obviously not an anomaly, as Jesus earns the reputation of being a "friend of tax collectors and sinners" (7:34). Thus it is quite ironic that, when the Pharisees and scribes grumble as they see tax collectors and sinners listening to Jesus (saying, "This man receives sinners"; 15:2), they provide the perfect short summary of Jesus' earthly ministry! He has indeed come "into the world" not only to receive sinners but to "save" them, even the worst of them ("the foremost"; 1 Tim. 1:15).

Whole-Bible Connections

A CELEBRATION MEAL. Repeatedly in the Bible, from Genesis to Revelation, the great joy that God has for his people is depicted in terms of a feast (e.g., Isa. 25:6; 30:29; Jer. 31:14; Luke 14:12–24). Then, at the Last Supper, Jesus institutes a shared meal that his disciples are to use to commemorate and celebrate his death until he returns (Luke 22:14–20; 1 Cor. 11:26). And when Jesus does return, we will partake of the most joyous feast *of* all time *for* all time: the marriage supper of the Lamb (Rev. 19:6–9). We will celebrate forever our forgiveness in Christ in the presence of our loving, triune God.

THE BEST ROBE. For the father in the parable of the prodigal to call his servant to "bring quickly the best robe" (Luke 15:22) highlights that the son has tattered or insufficient clothing. It also shows the father's extravagant love (he did not need to give the *best* robe). Scripture often uses clothing to shape a story. For example, in Genesis Joseph goes from being stripped of his many-colored robe to receiving Pharaoh's signet ring and being clothed in garments of fine linen, with a gold chain around his neck (Gen. 37:23; 41:42). At the other end of the Bible come the final pictures of royal clothing, as Christ himself is "clothed in a robe dipped in blood," "the armies of heaven" are "arrayed in fine linen," and the bride of Christ is granted "to clothe herself with fine linen, bright and pure" (Rev. 19:7–8, 13–14). We are robed in Christ's righteousness (see Zech. 3:3–9)—surely the best robe!

Theological Soundings

OUR SONSHIP IN CHRIST. Just as the prodigal son never stopped being the beloved son of his father, so we who are in Christ experience that same loving family fellowship. For all eternity Jesus, who is God the Son, has enjoyed complete unity and intimacy with the Father. He loves the Father completely and is completely loved by the Father, through the power of the Spirit, so that together the persons of the Trinity enjoy eternal, perfect joy in a loving relationship. We are enabled to call God "Father" by means of the Spirit of the Son, meaning that we are, through Jesus, enabled to enter into the same kind of relationship that Jesus himself has enjoyed for all eternity. God has brought us fully into his family.

AN IMPERISHABLE INHERITANCE. The prodigal squanders his inheritance. For those in Christ, that is not possible. We are promised, as Peter puts it, "an inheritance that is imperishable, undefiled, and unfading, kept in heaven" (1 Pet. 1:4). That inheritance is not today's money or our earthly family's land. Our inheritance is a sinless, resurrected existence in God's renewed heavens and earth (2 Pet. 3:13), the perfect promised land, where God himself will dwell with his people (Gen. 15:7; Deut. 1:8; Josh. 13:6) forever.

Personal Implications

Take time to reflect on the implications of Luke 15:11–32 for your own life today. Consider what you have learned that might lead you to praise God, repent of sin, and trust in his gracious promises. Make notes below on the *Personal Implications* for your walk with the Lord of the (1) *Gospel Glimpses*, (2) *Whole-Bible Connections*, (3) *Theological Soundings*, and (4) the passage as a whole.

1. Gospel Glimpses

2. Whole-Bible Connections

_____

_____

_____

_____

_____

3. Theological Soundings

_____

_____

_____

_____

_____

4. Luke 15:11–32

_____

_____

_____

_____

_____

As You Finish This Unit . . .

Take a moment now to ask for the Lord's blessing and help as you continue in this study of Jesus' parables. And take a moment also to look back through this unit of study, to reflect on a few key things that the Lord may be teaching you—and perhaps to highlight or underline these to review again in the future.

Definitions

[1] **Prodigal** – Someone who wastes resources or, in the case of the prodigal son, an inheritance, in irresponsible and excessive ways.

[2] **Tax collectors** – In the Gospels, Jews who collected taxes for Rome from their fellow countrymen. They were viewed as greedy, lawless traitors. They were also deemed unclean and a disgrace to their family and community and thus were excommunicated from the synagogue.

[3] **Repentance** – A complete change of heart and mind resulting in one's turning from sin to God. Repentance is both a command (Acts 3:19) and a gift (John 6:65; Acts 3:26; 5:31; 11:18; 2 Tim. 2:25). It both begins (justification) and marks (sanctification) the Christian life. Indeed, repentance is one of the main vehicles linking us to our Savior on a daily, even hourly, basis.

[4] **Forgiveness** – Release from guilt and the reestablishment of relationship. Forgiveness can be granted by God to humans (Luke 24:47; 1 John 1:9) and by humans to those who have wronged them (Matt. 18:21–22; Col. 3:13).

Week 6: The Rich Man and Lazarus

Luke 16:19–31

▲

The Place of the Passage

As Jesus continues his journey to Jerusalem, Luke records a number of the parables he tells on the way, including the parables of the mustard seed (Luke 13:18–19), the leaven (vv. 20–21), the lost sheep (15:4–6), the lost coin (vv. 8–9), and the prodigal son (vv. 15:11–32). Jesus will tell five more parables before he enters the holy city, including two parables related to the issue of wealth: the parable of the dishonest manager and the parable of the rich man and Lazarus.

The Big Picture

Following Jesus' famous saying "You cannot serve God and money" (Luke 16:13), he tells a parable about a man whose wealth-induced idolatry leads to God's eternal judgment.

Reflection and Discussion

Read through the complete passage for this study, Luke 16:19–31. Then think through and write your own notes on the following questions. (See *ESV Study Bible* notes on pages 1991–1992; online at www.esv.org.)

Both this parable and the previous one begin, "There was a rich man" (Luke 16:19; compare v. 1). Who is the audience for both parables?

How are the rich and riches depicted throughout Luke? Review Luke 1:53; 6:24; 8:14; 12:16–21; 14:12; 18:18–25; and especially 16:13–14. Are you surprised by what Jesus teaches? Based on what you know or have just learned about Jesus' teaching on these topics, how do you think the rich man in this parable will fare?

Read the story of Zacchaeus (Luke 19:1–10). Is it possible for a wealthy person to enter the kingdom of God? Now read the parable right after Zacchaeus's story (Luke 19:11–27). What light does the parable of the minas[1] shed on the theme of how to handle money?

Turn back to Luke 16:19–31. How is the rich man described? The poor man?

How should we act differently than the rich man did—in relation to both our use of money and our care for the poor?

When the poor man dies, he is "carried by the angels to Abraham's side"[2] (Luke 16:22). Considering what we have just learned about Jesus' teaching on the rich and riches in Luke, what is notable about introducing Abraham as the person in the place of comfort after death (see Gen. 13:2)?

The term *Hades*[3] is used, and some sort of depiction is given of what Christians commonly call heaven. Do you think this story is a real depiction of the afterlife? What might be a true depiction, and what might be an exaggeration to prove a point? (Our Lord Jesus was known for his use of hyperbole—intentional exaggerations to evoke an emotional response.)

When Abraham says to the rich man in torment, "Child, remember that you in your lifetime received your good things, and Lazarus in like manner bad things; but now he is comforted here, and you are in anguish" (Luke 16:25), is Jesus teaching that God's judgment is merely a reversal of fortunes? If someone has a prosperous and enjoyable earthly life, will he then have a deprived and awful afterlife? If not, what is at the heart of Jesus' teaching?

What is surprising about the damned man's dialogue with Abraham in Luke 16:25–30?

What is perhaps more surprising about Abraham's *answers* in Luke 16:29 and 31? What do those verses teach about Jesus' view of the Bible, which he labels "Moses and the Prophets"[4]?

Read through the following three sections on *Gospel Glimpses*, *Whole-Bible Connections*, and *Theological Soundings*. Then take time to consider the *Personal Implications* these sections have for you.

Gospel Glimpses

MERCY FOR THE NEEDY. Jesus' words and deeds throughout Luke contrast self-reliance with dependence on mercy: guests at a banquet vie for honor, while Jesus heals a man disfigured by disease (Luke 14:1–11); the host invites wealthy friends and family, when he should invite "the poor, the crippled, the lame, the blind" (v. 13; compare v. 21); a pitiless rich man endures torment, while a beggar "is comforted" (16:19–31). Jesus is teaching a twofold lesson: first, deep desire for saving mercy is fueled by recognition of our desperate need; second, receiving such mercy will make us eager to serve, rather than neglect, others in need.

SAVED FROM GOD'S WRATH. Lazarus is saved not only from a terrible earthly life but also from a horrid eternal judgment. This is true for all believers. Jesus, whom God "raised from the dead," is also the one who upon his return will "[deliver] us from the wrath to come" (1 Thess. 1:10). This pattern of salvation through judgment is found throughout the Bible, such as with Noah and the flood, the Passover, and the parting and closing of the Red Sea.

Whole-Bible Connections

GREED AND JUDGMENT. Found throughout the Bible is the tragic pattern of human greed that leads to God's judgment. In Joshua 7, Achan sins by stealing treasure devoted to destruction, bringing guilt and judgment on all Israel. In 2 Kings 5:15–27, Gehazi's lie to Naaman leads to Gehazi's suffering from leprosy. The early church was also tempted by greed and the misuse of spiritual power, such as in Ananias and Sapphira's dishonesty (Acts 5:1–11) and Simon the magician's attempted bribery (Acts 8:18–24). Most infamously, the greedy thief (see John 12:6) Judas Iscariot betrays Christ, the precious Son of God, for thirty pieces of silver (Matt. 26:14–15).

GOD'S HEART FOR THOSE SUFFERING. God cares for those suffering injustice and affliction. When Israel is enslaved in Egypt, God hears their cries, sees their affliction, and knows their suffering (Ex. 3:7). Then, after redeeming Israel from Egypt, God gives his people his law, replete with instructions to protect the poor, outsiders, and orphans and widows (Deut. 10:18–19; 15:7–11).

HELPING THE POOR. God exhorts his people repeatedly to care for the poor among them. This becomes a resounding theme throughout the early chapters of the Bible (e.g., Ex. 22:25; 23:11; Lev. 14:21), especially in Deuteronomy (e.g., Deut. 15:4–11; 24:12–15). It is later picked up frequently by the prophets (e.g., Isa. 58:7; Jer. 2:34; Amos 5:11). In the New Testament it is clearly an important theme as well (e.g., Acts 6:1; James 1:26–2:7; 5:1–6). The early church collects funds to provide supplies for believers facing poverty (Acts 11:27–30; Gal. 2:10).

James views mistreatment of the poor as a mark of unbelief (see James 2:1–6). The apostle Paul undertakes relief efforts for poor believers (e.g., Rom. 15:25–26; 1 Cor. 16:1–3), demonstrating the biblical principle that God cares about people's physical needs as well as their spiritual ones.

Theological Soundings

THE SUFFICIENCY OF SCRIPTURE. As Jesus makes absolutely clear in the parable of the rich man and Lazarus, the Hebrew Scriptures are sufficient to lead people to an understanding of salvation, and, if someone rejects God's written revelation ("If they do not hear Moses and the Prophets"), then he or she will even reject the miraculous works of God in history ("neither will they be convinced if someone should rise from the dead," Luke 16:31; see also 1 Cor. 15:1–3). God's Word, contained in both the Old and the New Testaments, is sufficient in all matters pertaining to salvation, as well as for doctrine and instruction in moral behavior.

THE INTERMEDIATE STATE. Before Christ returns to carry out final judgment, the souls of those who die will enter into what is known as the intermediate state—an experience of blessedness in God's presence for the souls of the faithful (heaven) and of punishment apart from him for unbelieving souls (hell[5]). While not all of its details should be pressed for doctrinal significance, Jesus' parable of the rich man and Lazarus (Luke 16:19–31) is foundational to our understanding of this interim state. The parable offers comfort to those who endure affliction now and an urgent warning to those who refuse the biblical call to repent, for "none may cross from there [hell] to us [in heaven]" (v. 26).

THE RESURRECTION. Christian doctrine affirms not only the resurrection of Christ but also a general resurrection in which, at Christ's second coming, the bodies and souls of the deceased will be reunited. (Those who are alive at Christ's return will receive resurrection bodies, though they will not have experienced death; see 1 Cor. 15:51–53.) Some will be raised "to everlasting life" and others "to shame and everlasting contempt" (Dan. 12:2). Jesus views the future glory of the "resurrection of the just" (Luke 14:14) as greater than any glory we could secure for ourselves in the present, and therefore as a motive for loving those who have nothing to offer us in return.

Personal Implications

Take time to reflect on the implications of Luke 16:19–31 for your own life today. Consider what you have learned that might lead you to praise God, repent of sin,

and trust in his gracious promises. Make notes below on the *Personal Implications* for your walk with the Lord of the (1) *Gospel Glimpses*, (2) *Whole-Bible Connections*, (3) *Theological Soundings*, and (4) the passage as a whole.

1. Gospel Glimpses

2. Whole-Bible Connections

3. Theological Soundings

4. Luke 16:19–31

As You Finish This Unit . . .

Take a moment now to ask for the Lord's blessing and help as you continue in this study of Jesus' parables. And take a moment also to look back through this unit of study, to reflect on a few key things that the Lord may be teaching you—and perhaps to highlight or underline these to review again in the future.

Definitions

[1] **Mina** – A unit of measurement of money, roughly equivalent to 1.25 pounds. A mina of silver was worth about three months' wages for a first-century laborer.

[2] **Abraham's side** – An image of what Christians often call "heaven." That after death believers are welcomed to "Abraham's side" (lit., "bosom") is symbolic of reception into fellowship with other believers already in heaven, particularly Abraham, the father of our faith and the one to whom God promised many offspring.

[3] **Hades** – In the New Testament, the abode of the dead prior to the second coming of Christ. Essentially equivalent to *Sheol* (commonly translated "the grave") in the Old Testament, it was associated with descriptions of a dark, prison-like place in the underworld, where the souls of the deceased resided.

[4] **Moses and the Prophets** – Moses (or "the law of Moses," or simply "the law") and the Prophets (from Samuel to Malachi) is shorthand for the entire Hebrew Bible or Old Testament.

[5] **Hell** – *Gehenna* in Greek, used to describe the trash heap outside of Jerusalem that was regularly set on fire. According to Jesus, hell is the place of "eternal fire" (Matt. 25:41), "eternal punishment" (25:46) and terrible suffering, where there will be "weeping and gnashing of teeth" (8:12; 13:42, 50; 22:13; 24:51; 25:30).

WEEK 7: TWO PARABLES ON PRAYER

Luke 18:1–14

▲

The Place of the Passage

Teaching on prayer is recorded in only a few places in Scripture, including in these two parables in Luke: the parable of the persistent widow (Luke 18:1–8) and the parable of the Pharisee and the tax collector (vv. 9–14). Jesus, a man of consistent communion with his Father through the Spirit, tells these parables to his followers shortly before he makes his final passion prediction (vv. 31–33) and enters Jerusalem to accomplish his mission (19:28).

The Big Picture

In these two parables on prayer, Jesus offers his disciples hope and encourages humility.

Reflection and Discussion

Read through the complete passage for this study, Luke 18:1–14. Then think through and write your own notes on the following questions. (See *ESV Study Bible* notes on pages 1994–1995; online at www.esv.org.).

What realities described in Luke 17:20–18:8 might cause us to be discouraged as we await Jesus' second coming ("when the Son of Man comes"; 18:8)?

In the first parable on prayer (Luke 18:1–8) why does the judge give in to the widow? What is the lesson for us (see v. 1)?

Why might Jesus have chosen a widow as a character? What does the widow want? How do her desires and actions relate to how God's people ("his elect"[1]) ought to pray "day and night" for God to "give justice"? What is the nature of this justice, and when will it come?

What do you make of Jesus' comment on the speed of God's justice for his elect? How about Jesus' comment on himself ("when the Son of Man comes . . ."; v. 8)? How is the judge like and unlike God?

The second parable (Luke 18:9–14) is traditionally named after its two characters, the Pharisee and the tax collector. From the New Testament, what do you know about the Pharisees? What about tax collectors?

What is totally different between the two men as they pray—in their attitudes, words, and actions?

Why does Jesus tell this second parable on prayer (see v. 9)?

Does self-righteousness[2] before God and contempt for others affect how God hears our prayers? Read Proverbs 15:8; 15:29; 28:9; Isaiah 59:1–2; James

5:16–18; and 1 Peter 3:10–12 and see how these other parts of Scripture shed light on this question.

Luke 18:9–14 also teaches us something about justification[3] (the tax collector "went down to his house *justified*," v. 14a, that is, declared right with God through God's forgiveness). How does this teaching on justification and what follows on humility ("Everyone who exalts himself will be humbled, but the one who humbles himself will be exalted"; v. 14b) relate to each other? And how does Jesus' end stress[4]—the two teachings in verse 14—offer additional insights on why Jesus tells the parable?

Read through the following three sections on *Gospel Glimpses, Whole-Bible Connections*, and *Theological Soundings*. Then take time to consider the *Personal Implications* these sections have for you.

Gospel Glimpses

SEEKING AND SAVING THE LOST. In this section of Luke's Gospel, Jesus repeatedly extends the blessings of salvation to those who are despised and treated "with contempt" (Luke 18:9)—including a Samaritan, children, a blind beggar, and Zacchaeus the tax collector. Unlike the Pharisee in this parable (vv. 10–14), Jesus embraces sinners who seek God's mercy. The Son of Man delights "to seek and to save the lost" (19:10)—even if it means being treated with contempt for our sake (18:32–33; 19:14).

DEEP FAITH, TRUE FRUIT. Faith that is born from a profound sense of sin, and thus from deep appreciation for God's mercy, will lead us to costly repentance and obedience. This is the message we learn through two tax collectors—one a sinner pleading for mercy in Jesus' parable (Luke 18:9–14) and the other a repentant Zacchaeus (19:1–10). By contrast, the Pharisee of Jesus' parable and the rich ruler of 18:18–23 boldly claim to obey God but are enslaved to the idols of pride and riches. Self-righteousness will never produce true repentance or obedience. These fruits grow only where the seed of God's unmerited favor to sinners is planted in the soil of desperate need.

Whole-Bible Connections

LORD, HAVE MERCY. The specific wording of the tax collector's prayer, "God, be merciful to me, a sinner!" (Luke 18:13), is unique in the Bible. However, similar expressions are found elsewhere, such as in the first line of David's prayer for forgiveness after his hideous sins of adultery and murder ("Have mercy on me, O God"; Ps. 51:1) and in one of Israel's songs of ascents that they sang as they journeyed to the temple to make atonement for their sins ("Have mercy upon us, O LORD, have mercy upon us"; Ps. 123:3). Whether as a confession of sin and plea for forgiveness or a cry for help (e.g., the two blind men's "Have mercy on us, Son of David," Matt. 9:27, or the Canaanite woman's supplication, "Have mercy on me, O Lord," 15:22), the prayer "Lord, have mercy" should be found often on our lips.

ANSWERED PRAYER. Jesus promises to answer prayer (John 14:12–14). Yet, we know from experience that God's responses to prayer can be rather mysterious. God knows infinitely more than we do. He has in mind not only our happiness or personal fulfillment but also our eternal good, linked to a grand plan involving countless interrelated people, events, purposes, and problems. James teaches that, sometimes, "You do not have, because you do not ask," while other times "You ask and do not receive, because you ask wrongly, to spend it on your passions" (James 4:2–3). God sometimes says no to our petitions for our own good, however mysterious that may be to us. On the other hand, God does seem to be attuned particularly to fervent prayers of the righteous (James 5:16–18). He can be honored by persistence in prayer, especially when one prays for something such as justice, as seen in the parable of the persistent widow (Luke 18:1–8).

Theological Soundings

JUSTIFICATION BY FAITH. In Jesus' parable of the Pharisee and the tax collector (Luke 18:9–14) we see three principles at the heart of the doctrine of

justification. (1) Boasting in human works—even religious disciplines—
is worthless before God. (2) Our only hope is to confess our need as sinners, casting ourselves on God's mercy. (3) The issue is not where we stand in comparison
to others but whether we are accepted by God. (The Greek term for "be merciful"
even implies securing mercy through the proper means, so that verse 13 may
allude to trust in the death of a sacrificial substitute.) Though we often associ-
ate it with the apostle Paul (Rom. 3:20–5:1; Gal. 2:16; 3:1–14), the doctrine of
justification by faith clearly has its roots in Jesus' teaching.

FINAL VINDICATION. There will be a vindication of God's people (the "justice"
we should pray for; Luke 18:7) at the end of time, when Christ will return in
great glory to claim his elect as his bride and to execute judgment against his
enemies. On that day there will be a definitive, comprehensive acknowledgment
that Jesus is Lord over all (see Phil. 2:10–11).

Personal Implications

Take time to reflect on the implications of Luke 18:1–14 for your own life today.
Consider what you have learned that might lead you to praise God, repent of sin,
and trust in his gracious promises. Make notes below on the *Personal Implications*
for your walk with the Lord of the (1) *Gospel Glimpses*, (2) *Whole-Bible Connections*,
(3) *Theological Soundings*, and (4) the passage as a whole.

1. Gospel Glimpses

2. Whole-Bible Connections

3. Theological Soundings

4. Luke 18:1–14

As You Finish This Unit . . .

Take a moment now to ask for the Lord's blessing and help as you continue in this study of Jesus' parables. And take a moment also to look back through this unit of study, to reflect on a few key things that the Lord may be teaching you—and perhaps to highlight or underline these to review again in the future.

Definitions

[1] **The elect** – People whom God has chosen from eternity for salvation. Or, as Paul summarizes in Romans 8, "God's elect" (8:33) are "those who are in Christ Jesus" (v. 1), for whom Christ died (v. 34), who have been adopted into God's family (v. 23), and who are "led by the Spirit of God" (v. 14) throughout life and are heirs of heaven, where in eternity they will "be glorified" with Christ (v. 17).

[2] **Self-righteousness** – The belief that one is acceptable before God because of one's own moral uprightness or human effort, rather than because of dependence on the grace of God. Self-righteousness begins with evaluating oneself in light of human standards rather than God's standards and is therefore typically accompanied by pride and a judgmental attitude toward others.

[3] **Justification** – The act of God's grace in bringing sinners into a new covenant relationship with himself and counting them as righteous before him through the forgiveness of their sins (see Rom. 3:20–26).

[4] **End stress** – The final line in a parable that summarizes or applies the whole narrative. (See the chart in Week 8 for examples of this.)

WEEK 8: THE UNFORGIVING SERVANT

Matthew 18:21–35

▲

This week we transition from Luke to Matthew. Yet, as in Luke, the events recorded in Matthew 18 take place on Jesus' journey to Jerusalem. On the way to his cross, Jesus teaches those who are part of his new community ("the church"; Matt. 18:17) about themes related to life together, including the greatness of servanthood, the covenant of marriage, and the forgiveness of sins.

The Big Picture

The parable of the unforgiving servant provides a summary of an essential part of Jesus' teaching on the radical kind of lifestyle needed for the church to live together in unity and love.

Reflection and Discussion

Read through the complete passage for this study, Matthew 18:21–35. Then think through and write your own notes on the following questions. (See *ESV Study Bible* notes on pages 1859–1860; online at www.esv.org.)

Why does Peter ask his question, "Lord, how often will my brother sin against me, and I forgive him? As many as seven times?" (Matt. 18:21)? Put differently, what in the preceding context prompts this question?

What does Peter's question reveal about his view of forgiveness? Do you view the forgiveness of those who sin against you in the same way?

How does Jesus' reply (18:22) reveal *his* view of forgiveness?

In the parable, the first servant's debt is ten thousand talents[1] (v. 24). What does this debt represent?

In light of this astronomical debt, what does the king decide to do? What does the servant do and say that changes the king's mind? How do the servant's actions help us better to understand repentance? How does the king's forgiveness of the debt help us better to understand God's mercy in Christ?

After the first servant is forgiven, what is shocking about how he treats his fellow servant, who owes him a lot less than he owed the king ("a hundred denarii";[2] Matt. 18:28)? Turn to Matthew 6:12. How does the first servant's behavior disobey Christ's clear instruction?

When the king (or "master"; Matt. 18:32) learns what has happened, how does he respond?

What do you think is being taught about the nature of the servant's punishment in verse 34? Does the master's anger symbolize God's wrath?

_____

_____

_____

_____

_____

_____

Is the man actually able to pay the debt? If not, does this represent eternal punishment in hell? Is he called a "servant" ("you wicked servant!"; v. 32) because he is still a forgiven Christian in God's sight, or does the statement indicate someone in the Christian community who is not a true believer (see Matt. 7:21–23)?

_____

_____

_____

_____

_____

Last week we defined *end stress* as "the final line in a parable that summarizes or applies the crux of the whole narrative." Below are examples of the end-stress summary maxims that Jesus uses in his parables. Why are these important? What is the specific significance of the end-stress summary in the parable of the unforgiven servant (Matt. 18:35; compare 6:14–15)?

Matthew 20:16	*So the last will be first, and the first last.*
Matthew 22:14	*For many are called, but few are chosen.*
Matthew 25:13	*Watch therefore, for you know neither the day nor the hour.*
Matthew 25:46	*And these will go away into eternal punishment, but the righteous into eternal life.*
Luke 10:37	*You go, and do likewise.*
Luke 12:21	*So is the one who lays up treasure for himself and is not rich toward God.*
Luke 14:11	*For everyone who exalts himself will be humbled, and he who humbles himself will be exalted.*

Luke 15:7	*There will be more joy in heaven over one sinner who repents than over ninety-nine righteous persons who need no repentance.*
Luke 18:14	*Everyone who exalts himself will be humbled, but the one who humbles himself will be exalted.*

Read through the following three sections on *Gospel Glimpses, Whole-Bible Connections,* and *Theological Soundings*. Then take time to consider the *Personal Implications* these sections have for you.

Gospel Glimpses

ASTRONOMICAL DEBT. Our Lord taught us to pray, "Forgive us our *debts*" (Matt. 6:12; or "sins," Luke 11:4). But how much have our sins indebted us to God? The parable of the unforgiving servant informs us. Our debt is the equivalent to the first servant's debt ("ten thousand talents"; Matt. 18:24), which in Jesus' day was the largest imaginable amount. The implications are obvious. Jesus puts to rest any notion of works-righteousness. It is an unfathomable debt! Who can repay it? The only way that such a debt, and the collective debt of all of God's people (a multitude no one can number), can be forgiven is if Jesus gives "his life as a ransom"[3] (20:28)—a full payment—for our past, present, and future sins. On the cross he paid the price. Jesus paid it all.

WE FORGIVE BECAUSE HE FIRST FORGAVE US. There is no mistaking Jesus' radical call to forgive others. We must forgive not seven but seventy-seven times, and always from the heart (Matt. 18:22, 35). In other words, there is really no limit. But where will we get the motivation to fuel this heart-level, boundless forgiveness? Jesus implies the answer with a story about a servant who was forgiven of an unfathomable debt but went on to demand repayment of a relatively minor sum. The point is that an unforgiving heart toward others is inconceivable for those who have been truly forgiven by God. When we see the kindhearted love of our Savior as the full weight of our sins is poured out on him at the cross, how can we then turn around and bitterly refuse to forgive someone else? The forgiveness of God, when truly grasped, transforms us to show this same forgiving grace to others (see Eph. 4:32).

Whole-Bible Connections

LORD. The word "master" in the parable is the Greek *kyrios,* most often translated "lord" throughout Matthew. In the Septuagint (the Greek translation of the Old Testament) it is used of Yahweh more than six thousand times! It is used of God the Father in the New Testament, but also of "the Lord Jesus" or "the Lord Jesus Christ." For example, when it is said of John the Baptist that he is preparing "the way of the Lord" (Matt. 3:3, quoting Isa. 40:3), this "Lord" is Jesus. Repeatedly, those who seek help from Jesus petition him as "Lord" (e.g., the leper who begs, "Lord, if you will, you can make me clean"; Matt. 8:2). Both Matthew's Gospel and the rest of the New Testament make clear that Jesus "has authority on earth to forgive sins" (9:6). And, to tie into this week's parable (and this week's second Gospel Glimpse), Christians "must forgive" one another "as the Lord [*kyrios*] has forgiven" them (Col. 3:13). When Paul refers to the "Lord," he is invariably referencing the Lord Jesus Christ.

FORGIVENESS IN CHRIST. Believers in the Old Testament received forgiveness for their sins by casting themselves upon God and pleading for his mercy through the sacrificial system and the ultimate sacrifice to which it pointed. Daily and yearly reminders of sin were built into the sanctuary and the sacrificial system (Heb. 7:27; 8:3). And in the new covenant Christ deals with sin once and for all (9:24–28), as God remembers our sins no more (8:12; see also Jer. 31:34). The Old Testament sacrifices pointed forward to the one who would offer himself as a sacrifice for sin (Isa. 53:10; Gal. 1:4). All who turn from their sins and trust in Jesus Christ experience God's forgiveness (Acts 2:38). In him alone our transgressions are removed, as far as the east is from the west (Ps. 103:12).

Theological Soundings

THE CHURCH AND DISCIPLINE. The Greek *ekklēsia* is often used in the Septuagint to render the Hebrew "assembly," and in the New Testament it is typically translated into English as "church." This word, found more than a hundred times in the New Testament, is used only three times in the Gospels, all in the Gospel of Matthew (Matt. 16:18; 18:17 [2x]). In Matthew 18:15–20 Jesus teaches about church discipline, outlining a process for responding to one disciple who sins against another. First, we must not ignore sin in the lives of Christian brothers and sisters: "If your brother sins against you, go and tell him his fault" (v. 15). Second, sins are to be dealt with first personally and privately. Only if there is a refusal to repent should the process progress to a conversation with two others. Then, if necessary, "the church," the whole believing community (vv. 15–17), should be consulted. Finally, the motivation throughout must be love, and the goal is restoration: "If he listens to you, you have gained your brother" (v. 15). The goal of church discipline for the wayward sinner is repentance and restoration, and the result is a joyful celebration (v. 13). In addition, church discipline protects the peace and purity of the church, signals the importance and seriousness of dealing with sin, and honors and glorifies Christ, the head of the church.

66

Personal Implications

Take time to reflect on the implications of Matthew 18:21–35 for your own life today. Consider what you have learned that might lead you to praise God, repent of sin, and trust in his gracious promises. Make notes below on the *Personal Implications* for your walk with the Lord of the (1) *Gospel Glimpses*, (2) *Whole-Bible Connections*, (3) *Theological Soundings*, and (4) the passage as a whole.

1. Gospel Glimpses

2. Whole-Bible Connections

3. Theological Soundings

4. Matthew 18:21–35

As You Finish This Unit . . .

Take a moment now to ask for the Lord's blessing and help as you continue in this study of Jesus' parables. And take a moment also to look back through this unit of study, to reflect on a few key things that the Lord may be teaching you—and perhaps to highlight or underline these to review again in the future.

Definitions

[1] **Talent** – In Old Testament times a unit of weight equaling about 75 pounds (34 kg). In New Testament times a unit of monetary reckoning (though not an actual coin), valued at about 6,000 drachmas, the equivalent of about 20 years' wages for a laborer. In approximate modern equivalents, if a laborer earned $15 per hour, at 2,000 hours per year he would earn $30,000 per year, and thus a talent would equal $600,000 (USD). Hence "ten thousand talents" hyperbolically represents an incalculable debt ($6 billion, in this example!).

[2] **Denarii** – Plural of denarius, a relatively small amount of money. A common laborer earned about one denarius per day.

[3] **Ransom** – A price paid to redeem, or buy back, someone who had become enslaved or something that had been lost to someone else. Jesus describes his ministry as serving others and giving his life as a ransom for many (Mark 10:45).

WEEK 9: THE LABORERS IN THE VINEYARD

Matthew 20:1–16

▲

The Place of the Passage

After Jesus taught the parable of the unmerciful servant, "He went away from Galilee and entered the region of Judea beyond the Jordan" (Matt. 19:1). Nearing Jerusalem, he continued his healing and preaching ministry. His preaching included a final parable (20:1–16) before he made his final passion prediction (20:17–19) and entered Jerusalem (21:10).

The Big Picture

The parable of the laborers in the vineyard has also been called the parable of the "injustice" of a generous God because God's grace is so shockingly generous that it might seem unfair to some.

> ## Reflection and Discussion

Read through the complete passage for this study, Matthew 20:1–16. Then think through and write your own notes on the following questions. (See *ESV Study Bible* notes on pages 1862–1863; online at www.esv.org.)

Read Matthew 19:13–30. What happens in the immediate narrative context? How does chapter 19 end (v. 30)? How does the parable of the laborers in the vineyard end (20:16)? What is the connection?

What does Jesus say immediately after this parable (Matt. 20:17–19)? Why is the placement of his prediction important?

Continuing on in the ensuing context, compare and contrast the request of the mother of the sons of Zebedee (Matt. 20:20–28) and the request of the two blind men (vv. 29–34). How do these accounts tie into the theme and the end stress of Jesus' parable (20:1–16)?

List every person, place, thing, and action included in this parable (20:1–16). Which of these elements likely has a second level of meaning? For each element that does, place a check mark on the righthand side of the table. Discuss your answers with a group if possible.

Detail	Second Level?

At the very least, it seems clear that the "master of the house" and the first (those hired "early in the morning"; Matt. 20:1) and last laborers ("those hired about the eleventh hour";[1] v. 9) have symbolic value. Whom do they symbolize, and what is the lesson we learn from their actions? (Complete this table before reading the *Gospel Glimpses*, *Whole-Bible Connections*, and *Theological Soundings* below.)

Detail	Referent
master of the house	
first-hired laborers	
last-hired laborers	

Are you sympathetic with the grumblers (see Matt. 20:11–12)? If so, is it because the lord of the vineyard seems irrational and eccentric and has broken some supposed rule of fair labor? Or is it because of some other reason? If so, what?

How did many pious religious people feel when Jesus extended grace to Zacchaeus (Luke 19:7) and the sinful woman (7:36–50)?

Think about Simeon and Anna, who patiently and obediently waited their whole lives for the coming Messiah, in contrast to the thief on the cross, who received the gift of salvation a moment before he died. Does such grace seem fair to you? Why or why not?

Is it fair that a criminal on death row who trusts in Christ the moment before his execution should receive the same eternal inheritance in heaven as someone who never experienced a day in which he or she did not know and love and seek to follow the Lord? Why or why not?

When do you find yourself begrudging and grumbling about God's generosity? What is an antidote for such a wrong attitude and action?

_____

_____

_____

_____

_____

_____

Read through the following three sections on *Gospel Glimpses, Whole-Bible Connections,* and *Theological Soundings.* Then take time to consider the *Personal Implications* these sections have for you.

Gospel Glimpses

UNDESERVING. According to Scripture, everyone deserves damnation; no one deserves salvation. With this in mind, we should be thankful that God is "not fair"—that is, he does not give us what we deserve. We undeserving sinners are given more than we deserve. Moreover, who is the subject of most of this parable's clauses? Who is talking? Acting? Taking the initiative? Calling and paying the workers? It is the owner of the vineyard—God, who will both do "whatever is right" (Matt. 20:4; he will do "no wrong," v. 13) and will also do beyond what is expected by calling those who have nothing, giving them work, and rewarding them for their labors on his behalf. Oh, the grace and goodness and love of God!

GRACE AND LABOR. As a theological undercurrent, Jesus teaches here that God's shockingly generous grace is not antithetical to kingdom labor. Notice that Jesus calls those in the kingdom of heaven "laborers" (Matt. 20:1, 2, 8; see also "worker" in v. 14) on earth who "worked" (v. 12). The one thing every hired laborer in this parable does is work, even if only for an hour. Jesus does not teach that God's grace takes idle people, lets them stay idle, and still rewards them with eternal life. Neither does he advocate salvation by good works, or hard work. Rather, he advocates that no one earns salvation or is owed salvation based on good works or hard work or much work, but those who are chosen by grace are given work to do, do that work, and are rewarded for it.

Whole-Bible Connections

GRUMBLING. The word "grumbled" (Matt. 20:11) should remind us of Israel's grumblings in the wilderness, and Jesus uses the word to make an important thematic connection (and correction!): we must not be like the exodus generation, which was saved from slavery, from the rule of Pharaoh, and from the Red Sea, only to die without inheriting the promise. Those people died because they never got past their grumbling. They were never grateful for grace. If we look at all of the references to grumbling in the Bible, we will realize that, to God, grumbling is as deadly a sin as adultery or murder. The grumblers' camp is not a good camp in which to be, as is made clear by various admonitions in the New Testament (see Phil. 2:14; James 5:9; 1 Pet. 4:9).

LABORING IN THE VINEYARD. The laborers of the vineyard are members of the kingdom of heaven. The work of the vineyard then represents Christian work, either more broadly (the specific work the Lord has given us to do) or more specifically as gospel work (harvesting those people God has saved through the message of his gospel). Due to the harvest/laborer language in Matthew 9:37–38 (the only other place in which the terms "laborers" and "harvest" are used together), the latter interpretation is more likely, especially as the parable is addressed to Peter and his question regarding reward for his sacrificial service as an apostle (19:27). The vineyard, or specifically the harvest of that vineyard, initially represents the people of Israel (see Isaiah 5; Jeremiah 12) but then expands to include *new tenants*—believing Jews and Gentiles—from "all nations" (Matt. 28:19; see also Acts 1:8 and the entire book of Acts!).

Theological Soundings

THE EVIL EYE. The question "Do you begrudge my generosity?" (Matt. 20:15) can be rendered literally "Is your eye bad because I am good?" The focus is on the eye, the "evil eye." These workers give God the evil eye. They are not seeing him as good or generous. This is their problem, which is too often our problem as well. Self-interest, a lack of compassion for others, or a misunderstanding of the nature of grace distorts clear vision. We see what is good as evil, what is compassionate as cruel, what is generous as tightfisted.

ESCHATOLOGICAL JUDGMENT. The denarius (Matt. 20:2) represents the gift of final salvation (the "eternal life" the rich ruler desired; see Luke 18:18). Put differently, it represents the eschatological judgment of the just. The money is given at the end of the day. This fits Old Testament labor laws (Lev. 19:13; Deut. 24:14–15) and also fits New Testament eschatology. Christians are saved now—the moment they trust in Christ—but will be saved also in the future, on the day of reckoning, when Christ's work will be accounted as payment in full on behalf of all those who believe.

Personal Implications

Take time to reflect on the implications of Matthew 20:1–16 for your own life today. Consider what you have learned that might lead you to praise God, repent of sin, and trust in his gracious promises. Make notes below on the *Personal Implications* for your walk with the Lord of the (1) *Gospel Glimpses*, (2) *Whole-Bible Connections*, (3) *Theological Soundings*, and (4) the passage as a whole.

1. Gospel Glimpses

2. Whole-Bible Connections

3. Theological Soundings

4. Matthew 20:1–16

As You Finish This Unit . . .

Take a moment now to ask for the Lord's blessing and help as you continue in this study of Jesus' parables. And take a moment also to look back through this unit of study, to reflect on a few key things that the Lord may be teaching you—and perhaps to highlight or underline these to review again in the future.

Definitions

[1] **Eleventh hour** – Term used twice by Jesus in this parable (Matt. 20:6, 9) to indicate "the latest possible time" (Merriam-Webster) before it is too late. The Gospel writers used the typical Jewish time divisions of the first century (e.g., the third hour is roughly our 9:00 AM; the sixth hour is midday; the ninth is roughly our 3:00 PM; etc.). The eleventh hour would therefore be nearly the end of the workday.

Week 10: The Tenants

Mark 12:1–12

The Place of the Passage

Jesus has announced his imminent suffering and death. And now the end has drawn near. In Mark 11:1–12:44 Jesus enters Jerusalem triumphantly, cleanses the temple,[1] and authoritatively teaches both opponents and disciples. In response to such actions and teachings, the opposition of the religious authorities heightens.

The Big Picture

In perhaps his most provocative parable Jesus speaks clearly of his identity, mission, and predicted rejection.

> ## Reflection and Discussion

Read through the complete passage for this study, Mark 12:1–12. Then think through and write your own notes on the following questions. (See *ESV Study Bible* notes on pages 1919–1920; online at www.esv.org.)

The parable of the tenants is one of the few parables told in all of the Synoptic Gospels (Mark 12:1–12; Matt. 21:33–46; Luke 20:9–18). Skim through Mark 11:1–33; Matthew 21:1–32; and Luke 19:28–20:8. What is found in the preceding context of Matthew that is not found in Mark or Luke? Whom do you think the character in Matthew 21:30, or the "you" in verse 32, represents?

What is the reaction to this parable in Mark 12:12–13? From the context, who are the "they" of these two verses (see also Matt. 21:45)?

In parable interpretation, it is important to understand quotations and possible allusions[2] from the Old Testament. For example, how does Isaiah 5:1–7 shed light on this parable?

This parable contains five characters: the owner of the vineyard, his tenants, his servants, his beloved son, and his other (new) tenants. Whom does each of these symbolize?

List all of the owner's actions in Mark 12:1–6. What do we learn about God from these actions?

List all of the *tenants'* actions in Mark 12:2–8. What do we learn from these actions about the people whom the tenants symbolize? How do their actions relate to the parable of the two sons in Matthew 21:28–32?

How do these actions, including their action toward the owner's son, retell the story of salvation history in a very condensed form?

How does the owner react to the tenants' behavior (Mark 12:9)? See also what Matthew adds in his record (Matt. 21:41, 43–44). What do these actions represent? What do these actions teach us about God?

Matthew also speaks of the vineyard owner's giving the vineyard "to a people [*ethnos*, a collective singular, often translated "nations"] producing its fruits" (Matt. 21:43). What is the significance of this description?

Besides bearing fruit, how should we respond to this parable? How does it challenge us to think, feel, and act differently?

In Mark 12:10–11 Jesus quotes from Psalm 118:22–23, verses that originally spoke of the nation of Israel. Jesus appropriately and authoritatively applies it to himself. How does Peter in Acts 4:5–11 explain and apply these verses? How about Paul in Ephesians 2:11–21?

Read through the following three sections on *Gospel Glimpses, Whole-Bible Connections*, and *Theological Soundings*. Then take time to consider the *Personal Implications* these sections have for you.

Gospel Glimpses

PATIENT, COSTLY LOVE. One of the lessons taught by Jesus' parable of the wicked tenants is God's patient, costly love for sinners. God, depicted as a vineyard owner, has every right to destroy his people when they reject prophets and other leaders who call them to faithfulness. Instead, he patiently reaches out to his people again and again. While justice demands that all pay the price for their sins, God pays an even greater price—ultimately sending his "beloved son" to die. Surely the response to such love should be repentant, joyful thanksgiving!

THE SENT SON. The word "sent" is used five times in the parable of the tenants. God sent "prophets and wise men" (Matt. 23:34), one after the other, century after century, many of whom were persecuted and some of whom were murdered. Finally, as the greatest act of love in world history, he sent his "beloved son" (Mark 12:6; see also John 17:23), who was beaten and killed. Other New Testament authors employ the word "send" or "sent" (*apostellō*) to summarize aspects of the attributes of God and the nature of Jesus' mission. In "the fullness of time" God "sent forth his Son," who was "born of woman" and "born under the law, to redeem those who were under the law" and to adopt them "as sons" (Gal. 4:4–5). God "condemned sin in the flesh" by "sending his own Son in the likeness of sinful flesh and for sin" (Rom. 8:3). Because God "loved us" he "sent his only Son into the world" as "the propitiation for our sins" and "so that we might live through him" (1 John 4:9–10; see also John 17:3). "The Father has sent his Son to be the Savior of the world" (1 John 4:14).

Whole-Bible Connections

THE REJECTED REDEEMER. As the rejected cornerstone[3] (Mark 12:10), Jesus represents the culmination of a larger biblical pattern in which God raises up leaders who are then scorned by his people. Acts 7:1–53 reminds us that two of the Old Testament's greatest heroes were men who had been rejected by their fellow Israelites: Joseph was sold into slavery, yet he later delivered Israel from famine; Moses became an exile from Egypt, yet he returned to free the nation from slavery. This pattern is intensified in Jesus: although Jesus was crucified by "sinful men" (Luke 24:7), God "exalted him . . . as Leader and Savior, to give repentance to Israel and forgiveness of sins" (Acts 5:31).

THE STONE. Jesus' conclusion of the parable of the tenants, as recorded in Matthew and Luke, includes an allusion to Daniel 2:34: "And the one who falls on this stone will be broken to pieces; and when it falls on anyone, it will crush him" (Matt. 21:44). In the passage from Daniel, Nebuchadnezzar saw a vision of a stone that "was cut out by no human hand" and "struck the image [from the king's vision] on its feet of iron and clay, and broke them in pieces" (Dan. 2:34); the stone "broke in pieces the iron, the bronze, the clay, the silver, and the gold" (v. 45). The irony is that it is idolatrous Israel, not Babylon,[4] whom God judges in this parable. Soon after Jesus' access-opening death, the temple will be razed to the ground. Yet, out of the rubble, a new and everlasting stone is put in place. That stone is Christ crucified, risen, and exalted—which will indeed be "the Lord's doing" and "marvelous" in the eyes of the apostles and still in our eyes today! The stone that the builders (or "tenants," the Jewish leaders) rejected has become the foundational stone of the new temple. And this stone either saves or crushes. The stone either stays in place as the cornerstone on which we build our fruitful lives or is pushed out of place to become a stumbling stone that rolls over and crushes to dust all who oppose it (see Isa. 8:14–15; Dan. 2:34–35).

Theological Soundings

FRUITFUL. According to the prophets, Israel was called to be a fruitful tree but failed. God spoke through Jeremiah, saying, "When I would gather them, declares the LORD, there are no grapes on the vine, nor figs on the fig tree; even the leaves are withered" (Jer. 8:13; see also Hos. 9:10, 16; Joel 1:7). And Isaiah, using the metaphor of a vineyard (Isa. 5:1), retells Israel's history from its initial "planting" in Canaan to its continual failure to bear righteous fruit (5:1–7). While Isaiah sees destruction coming in the future (5:5–6), the psalmist later writes from the midst of that judgment and pleads for God to "have regard for this vine" (Ps. 80:14). When Jesus arrives in Jerusalem, he sandwiches his cleansing of the temple between the two halves of the cursing of a barren fig tree, an act signifying judgment upon Israel's fruitlessness (Mark 11:12–22). Jesus himself, however, goes to the cross—is judged and treated as "fruitless"—so that fallen people like us can become the fruitful trees we were meant to be (John 15:1–8).

Personal Implications

Take time to reflect on the implications of Mark 12:1–12 for your own life today. Consider what you have learned that might lead you to praise God, repent of sin, and trust in his gracious promises. Make notes below on the *Personal Implications*

for your walk with the Lord of the (1) *Gospel Glimpses*, (2) *Whole-Bible Connections*, (3) *Theological Soundings*, and (4) the passage as a whole.

1. Gospel Glimpses

2. Whole-Bible Connections

3. Theological Soundings

4. Mark 12:1–12

> ## As You Finish This Unit . . .

Take a moment now to ask for the Lord's blessing and help as you continue in this study of Jesus' parables. And take a moment also to look back through this unit of study, to reflect on a few key things that the Lord may be teaching you—and perhaps to highlight or underline these to review again in the future.

Definitions

[1] **Temple** – A building set aside as holy because God's presence is manifested there in a special way. Solomon built the first temple of the Lord in Jerusalem, to replace the portable tabernacle. This temple was later destroyed by the Babylonians, rebuilt and expanded, and then destroyed again by the Romans. Jesus is the true and final temple (John 2:18–22), and all those united to him through faith become part of this temple (Eph. 2:20–22).

[2] **Allusion** – A reference, sometimes by means of a quotation, to past history or literature.

[3] **Cornerstone** – Either the keystone/capstone of an arch or, more likely, the large stone at the corner of a building's foundation (see Isa. 28:16; Eph. 2:20).

[4] **Babylon** – The nation that God raised up to fulfill his covenant warnings of destruction on Israel because of her long history of disobedience (Lev. 26:33, 29; Deut. 4:27; 28:64). Babylon destroyed Jerusalem, burned the temple, and executed or exiled the Israelites in 586 BC. Babylon is also used metaphorically in Revelation to represent Rome and thus all evil rule in the world, which Christ will come to judge once and for all time.

WEEK 11: THE WEDDING FEAST

Matthew 22:1–14

▲

The Place of the Passage

Matthew 16:21 is a turning point in Jesus' ministry, for "from that time Jesus began to show his disciples that he must go to Jerusalem and suffer many things . . . and be killed, and on the third day be raised." The focus in Matthew 21–23 is on the religious leaders' opposition to Jesus as he arrives in Jerusalem. Jesus responds by rebuking them in the form of parables (21:28–22:14), debating with them (22:15–45), and pronouncing woes upon them (23:1–39). This prepares us for the coming chapters, in which the conflict will climax with the crucifixion.

The Big Picture

In Matthew 21–23, Jesus arrives in Jerusalem amid praise but soon engages in conflict with the Jewish leaders about his own identity and their rejection of him.

Reflection and Discussion

Read through the complete passage for this study, Matthew 22:1–14. Then think through and write your own notes on the following questions. (See *ESV Study Bible* notes on pages 1868–1869; online at www.esv.org.)

The introduction to this parable reads, "And again Jesus spoke to them in parables." Who is Jesus' audience ("them")? What other parables has he told in this setting?

Jesus' parable of the wedding feast in Matthew 22:1–14 is a parable of judgment. Has Jesus said or made other verbal or physical judgments in Matthew 21? Does he do so in Matthew 23? What are they?

In Jesus' parable (Matt. 22:1–14) he compares the "kingdom of heaven" to a "king who gave a wedding feast[1] for his son" and then "sent his servants to call those who were invited to the wedding feast" (vv. 2, 3). What does the king symbolize? His son? The wedding feast? If able, give support for your answers from elsewhere in the New Testament.

List the actions of the king (see Matt. 22:2, 3, 4). What do these actions reveal about his character?

Whom do the king's servants symbolize? How about those who were invited? How did they respond to the king's invitation and servants? What does their rejection of the invitation symbolize? Do you find that today people still respond in similar ways when invited to receive the good news about Jesus?

In Luke 14:15–24 Jesus tells another parable about God's inviting people to a "great banquet," his sending out a servant to invite "many" people to it (v. 16), and their rejecting the invitation (vv. 18–20). Read the end of that parable (vv. 21–24) and then Matthew 22:7–14. How are the two conclusions similar? How are they different?

In Matthew 22:7, how does the king respond to those who reject his invitation? Whom do "his troops" and "those murderers" symbolize, and what does the destruction of "their city" represent in history?

The second half of the parable (Matt. 22:8–14) has a structure similar to that of the first half (vv. 1–7): invitations (vv. 2, 3a, 4; 8, 9, 11, 12a); responses (vv. 3b, 10, 12c), and judgments (vv. 7, 13b). We also find two of the same characters: the king and his servants. However, in the second half two new characters are introduced: "guests" (v. 10) and "the attendants" (v. 13). Based on their actions, do you have any educated guesses as to their identities? What are the reasons for your guesses?

How is the "man who had no wedding garment" judged? And *why* is he judged? Or, put differently, what does the "wedding garment" represent? If you need help, go to Matthew 25:31–46; Galatians 3:27; Colossians 3:12–14; or Revelation 7:9, 13–14, 19:7–8 for answers.

Jesus' final statement ("For many are called, but few are chosen"; Matt. 22:14) can be confusing. The Greek word translated "called" is *klētos*, while "chosen" is from *eklektos*. What is confusing is that *eklektos* is translated elsewhere as "called" (e.g., Rom. 8:30). To Paul, the "called" are the predestined elect—those who are effectively called. In Matthew 22:1–14 what does Jesus mean by the word "called" (*klētos*)? Hint: Jesus uses a related word (*kaleō*, translated "call" or "invite") elsewhere in this parable (vv. 3, 8, 9, 10). And what does he mean by the word "chosen" (*eklektos*) both here in verse 14 and also in 24:22, 24, 31 (there translated "elect")?

Read through the following three sections on *Gospel Glimpses*, *Whole-Bible Connections*, and *Theological Soundings*. Then take time to consider the *Personal Implications* these sections have for you.

Gospel Glimpses

UNWORTHY WORTHINESS. Jesus compares his kingdom to a wedding feast that a king throws for his son. Those first invited refuse to come and are therefore pronounced "not worthy" (Matt. 22:8). The king then sends his invitation to the streets, and many come to the feast, "both bad and good" (v. 10). Apparently unworthiness is not about being bad, for those who finally come to the feast are "both bad and good." Likewise, worthiness is not about being good, for the first invitees are judged unworthy simply because they refuse the invitation. Worthiness here is based not on moral performance but on a willingness to come to the king's party. In other words, worthiness is about a willingness to receive grace. The kingdom's entrance invitation does not say, "Are you good enough?" but asks, "Whether good or bad, are you willing to come?"

Whole-Bible Connections

COSMIC MARRIAGE. In the history of salvation, the initial relationship God establishes between Adam and Eve is that of marriage (Gen. 2:24; Matt. 19:4–5). God identifies Israel as his wife on the basis of their covenantal relationship (Hos. 2:2, 16, 19). Yet Israel is found guilty of adultery as she seeks after idols (Ex. 34:15; Jer. 2:35–36; Hos. 3:1). This cosmic marriage results in divorce as the wife turns to other lovers (Isa. 50:1; Jer. 3:8; Hos. 2:2). The Lord alone makes provisions to receive back his wife (Hos. 1:10–11; 2:14–15). In comparing "the kingdom of heaven . . . to a king who gave a wedding feast for his son" (Matt. 22:2) and calling the church his "bride," Christ intends for earthly marriage to display the hope of the heavenly marriage (Eph. 5:23, 27, 31–32). When the people of God are glorified, we all will enjoy marriage to Christ, rejoice in the marriage supper of the Lamb (Rev. 19:7, 9), and enjoy the consummation of the eternal marriage forever and ever (Rev. 21:1–4).

Theological Soundings

GOD'S ANGER AND WRATH. In this parable we read of the king's anger ("the king was angry") and wrath ("he sent his troops" to those who did not accept his invitation, and his troops "destroyed those murderers and burned their city"; Matt. 22:7); the king has those who attend the wedding "without a wedding garment . . . cast . . . into the outer darkness" (vv. 12, 13). This parabolic story is symbolic of God's holy anger and divine wrath. While the doctrine of God's holy anger and divine wrath is certainly a difficult one for many people to contemplate, it is presented throughout the Bible as the just and necessary response to evil and as one aspect of God's righteous character. His wrath is his settled, judicial disposition against sin and evil. It flows out of his goodness, for he is unwilling to let evil and injustice go unanswered. God's wrath ultimately highlights his glory, for it demonstrates his commitment to holiness and righteousness. And it measures the depth of his love, for he has determined to bear his own wrath fully in the person of his Son for the sake of his elect. It is this fury of God's anger against human sin that Jesus suffers for us on the cross in order to save us (people born "children of wrath"; Eph. 2:3) from his judgment.

GENERAL AND EFFECTIVE CALLING. That many (Gk. *polloi*) are called means that many have been invited to the wedding feast. But not all those invited are actually the ones who are supposed to be there, because *few* are chosen. This has been described as the doctrine of "general calling": the gospel is proclaimed to all people everywhere, both those who will believe and those who will not. However, Paul also mentions another kind of calling, an effective calling from God that comes powerfully to individuals and always brings a positive response. When the gospel is proclaimed, only *some* are effectively called—that is, those who are the elect, who respond with true faith (1 Cor. 1:24, 26–28). This is consistent with Jesus' statement that "few are chosen," for the ones "chosen" (Gk. *eklektos*) are "the elect," a term used by Jesus to refer to his true disciples (compare Matt. 11:27; 24:22, 24, 31).

Personal Implications

Take time to reflect on the implications of Matthew 22:1–14 for your own life today. Consider what you have learned that might lead you to praise God, repent of sin, and trust in his gracious promises. Make notes below on the *Personal Implications* for your walk with the Lord of the (1) *Gospel Glimpses*, (2) *Whole-Bible Connections*, (3) *Theological Soundings*, and (4) the passage as a whole.

1. Gospel Glimpses

----

2. Whole-Bible Connections

3. Theological Soundings

4. Matthew 22:1–14

> ## As You Finish This Unit . . .

Take a moment now to ask for the Lord's blessing and help as you continue in this study of Jesus' parables. And take a moment also to look back through this unit of study, to reflect on a few key things that the Lord may be teaching you—and perhaps to highlight or underline these to review again in the future.

Definitions

[1] **Wedding feast** – In this case, a countrywide seven-day marriage celebration (see Gen. 29:27; Judg. 14:12), that would feature singing (Jer. 7:34; Song of Solomon) as well as food and wine (John 2:1–11).

Week 12: Three Parables on Christ's Return

Matthew 25

The conflict of Matthew 21–23 leads to Jesus' pronouncing "woes" upon the religious leaders. Then in Matthew 24 Jesus announces a coming judgment against the temple and various trials that will characterize the age until his return. This leads to a series of parables that Jesus delivers to encourage his people to be prepared for his return.

The Big Picture

In the Olivet Discourse (Matthew 24–25) Jesus announces judgment against Jerusalem, teaches about coming trials, and motivates his followers to prepare for his glorious return.

> ### Reflection and Discussion

Read through the complete passage for this study, Matthew 25. Then think through and write your own notes on the following questions. (See *ESV Study Bible* notes on pages 1876–1877; online at www.esv.org.)

Read Matthew 24:1–3. Where is Jesus sitting, and what is he looking at? After he predicts the destruction of the temple (v. 2), what question do his disciples ask him?

Their question suggests that the disciples are confused. They think that the destruction of the temple must coincide with the end of the age.[1] How does Jesus in Matthew 24:3–51 clear up the confusion? More specifically, note a few key details about what will happen (a) when the temple is being destroyed and (b) when Jesus returns. List the commands he gives. What commands apply only to the Christians of the first century? What commands apply to us today?

In Matthew 24:36–25:46 (and through five parables!) Jesus instructs the church to prepare for his *parousia*[2] (or return). Each parable uniquely fills out the theme of preparedness for Jesus' return. What is the point of the first parable (24:42–44)? What does "stay awake" (v. 42) mean, and how do 1 Thessalonians

5:1–8; 1 Peter 4:7; and 2 Peter 3:10–13 fill out our understanding of how we are to live in light of Christ's second coming?

The key characters in the parable of the ten virgins (25:1–13) are the bridegroom, the wise virgins, and the foolish virgins. What lesson do we learn from each about the nature of Jesus' second coming and the right and wrong responses to that reality?

What is most surprising about the parable of the ten virgins? How do you make sense of that surprise?

How does the parable of the talents (Matt. 25:14–30) answer the question "How does Jesus want us to live in light of his return?"

How does the parable of the sheep and the goats (Matt. 25:31–46) answer the question "How does Jesus want us to live in light of his return?"

The original audience for the parable of the wedding feast (Matt. 22:1–14) certainly included the Jewish religious leaders. It makes sense that Jesus would tell a parable of judgment so they might repent before it is too late (as some will do; see Matt. 27:57; Acts 6:7). But why would Jesus tell parables of judgment, or possible judgment, to "his disciples" (Matt. 24:1; see also 1 Corinthians 10; Gal. 5:19–23)?

Read Matthew 25:10, 20–23, 34. What are the blessings that good and faithful Christians will receive from Jesus on judgment day? How should such blessings or rewards motivate you to press on in the Christian life?

Read through the following three sections on *Gospel Glimpses*, *Whole-Bible Connections*, and *Theological Soundings*. Then take time to consider the *Personal Implications* these sections have for you.

Gospel Glimpses

COMMENDED FAITHFULNESS. When the first two servants invest and multiply the money their master has given them, the master responds, "Well done, good and faithful servant" (Matt. 25:21, 23). This is a picture of the gracious and generous commendation Jesus will give all of his servants when he returns. The apostle Paul likewise affirms, "Each one will receive his commendation from God" (1 Cor. 4:5; see Rom. 2:29; Heb. 11:2, 4, 5, 39). This is over-the-top generosity to sinners. All of our works are done in response to and empowered by God and his grace (Rom. 2:26–29; Gal. 5:22; Phil. 2:13). Moreover, they are also imperfect and require the sacrifice of Jesus for them to be acceptable. Yet God will commend his people for the very things he has enabled them to do! This is why his praise of us will ultimately resound not to our glory but to his.

THE GIFT OF THE KINGDOM. At the final judgment, Jesus will say, "Come, you who are blessed by my Father, inherit the kingdom prepared for you from the foundation of the world" (Matt. 25:34). An inheritance is not worked for or earned; it is received. While Jesus points to the selfless service of those who will ultimately be saved, the ultimate reason for their entrance into his kingdom is grace. It is a gift. The sheep's surprise at hearing of their own works demonstrates that none of these works was done for the sake of repayment (25:37–39). With Jesus, earning is out of the question. He gives his kingdom on terms of grace.

Whole-Bible Connections

CHRIST, THE BRIDEGROOM. Marriage was instituted by God at creation (Gen. 2:24), and it serves as a reflection of the covenant relationship between God and his people (e.g., Isa. 54:5). In the Old Testament, Israel is frequently depicted as God's "bride" (e.g., Isa. 62:4–5; Jer. 2:2; Hos. 2:16–20), and he seeks to delight in his restored people "as the bridegroom rejoices over the bride" (Isa. 62:5; also 65:19). In the New Testament John the Baptist calls Jesus the bridegroom (John 3:29), which identifies Jesus as Israel's long-awaited king and Messiah. Jesus likewise uses the title "bridegroom" of himself (Mark 2:19). Jesus is the ultimate bridegroom, forever united with his bride—the church (Eph. 5:22–33). He so loves the church that he has died for her and continues to restore and sanctify her (vv. 25–32). One day "the Bride, the wife of the Lamb" will be wed to Jesus, the Lamb of God, and there will be great rejoicing, feasting, and celebration (Rev. 21:9; see also v. 2). "Blessed are those who are invited to the marriage supper of the Lamb" (19:9).

THE DESTRUCTION OF THE TEMPLE. In 586 BC the Babylonians destroyed Jerusalem and its temple (2 Kings 25; Pss. 74:3, 7; 79:1). According to 2 Kings

23:27 this event represented God's judgment in casting off his people, removing them from his sight; according to 2 Kings 24:20 it is an expression of his anger and his desire to remove them from his presence. In AD 70 God also expressed his anger over Israel's faithlessness and fruitlessness, when Herod's temple was destroyed by the Roman regiments ("Jerusalem surrounded by armies"; Luke 21:20). And, as Jesus predicted, every "stone" was "thrown down" (Mark 13:2). Of course, now in Christ—our Immanuel—and through his Holy Spirit who dwells within God's people (Eph. 2:13–22) Christians have permanent access into God's presence, both in this life (John 15:11–16) and in the life to come (Rev. 22:2–4).

Theological Soundings

ESCHATOLOGY. Theologians use the word *eschatology* to refer to the study of the "last things" or "end times." According to the New Testament the "end times" began when Jesus arrived on the scene to start his ministry and so to begin the fulfillment of Old Testament hopes and promises. Yet Matthew 24–25 points us forward to the time of their complete fulfillment. We still await the glorious second coming of Jesus (24:36), the gathering of all believers to be with him (24:31), the final judgment (25:31–46), and the separation of all people for either eternal punishment or eternal life (25:34, 41, 46).

MIXED CHURCH. The church is a mixed body comprising wheat and weeds, sheep and goats, two sets of servants, wise and foolish virgins. At the final judgment the true believers will be separated from the false. This will include those who identify with the church ("servants"; Matt. 25:14) and confess proper Christology (calling Jesus, "Lord, lord"; Matt 25:11) but who do not do the Father's will and who therefore do not truly know Jesus and thus are not known by him (v. 12; compare "those who do not know God and . . . do not obey the gospel of our Lord Jesus," 2 Thess. 1:8). The "wicked and slothful" (Matt. 25:26) will suffer "eternal punishment" (v. 46) when Christ returns and "cast[s them] into the outer darkness" (v. 30; "into the eternal fire," v. 41), a "place" where "there will be weeping and gnashing of teeth" (v. 30).

Personal Implications

Take time to reflect on the implications of Matthew 25 for your own life today. Consider what you have learned that might lead you to praise God, repent of sin, and trust in his gracious promises. Make notes below on the *Personal Implications* for your walk with the Lord of the (1) *Gospel Glimpses*, (2) *Whole-Bible Connections*, (3) *Theological Soundings*, and (4) the passage as a whole.

1. Gospel Glimpses

2. Whole-Bible Connections

3. Theological Soundings

4. Matthew 25

As You Finish Studying Jesus' Parables . . .

We rejoice with you as you complete this study of Jesus' parables! May what you have learned go with you day by day throughout your life. Now we would greatly encourage you to study the Word of God on a weekly, and even daily, basis. To continue your study of the Bible we invite you to consider other books in the Knowing the Bible series and to visit www.knowingthebibleseries.org.

Lastly, take a moment again to look back through this study. Review again the notes that you have written, and the things that you have highlighted or underlined. Reflect again on the key themes that the Lord has been teaching you about himself and about his Word. May these things become a treasure for you throughout your life—this we pray in the name of the Father, and the Son, and the Holy Spirit. Amen.

Definitions

[1] **The end of the age** – The day of Jesus' second coming and final judgment of the righteous and the wicked. The phrase is used only in the Gospel of Matthew (13:39, 40; 24:3, 28:20).

[2] **Parousia** – The Greek word for "arrival," "coming," or "presence." It is used forty-four times in the New Testament (e.g., Matt. 24:37, 39), often in relation to Christ's second coming.

KNOWING THE BIBLE STUDY GUIDE SERIES

Experience the *Grace* of God in the *Word* of God, Book by Book

Series Volumes

- Genesis
- Exodus
- Leviticus
- Numbers
- Deuteronomy
- Joshua
- Judges
- Ruth and Esther
- 1–2 Samuel
- 1–2 Kings
- 1–2 Chronicles
- Ezra and Nehemiah
- Job
- Psalms
- Proverbs
- Ecclesiastes
- Song of Solomon

- Isaiah
- Jeremiah
- Lamentations, Habakkuk, and Zephaniah
- Ezekiel
- Daniel
- Hosea
- Joel, Amos, and Obadiah
- Jonah, Micah, and Nahum
- Haggai, Zechariah, and Malachi
- Matthew
- Mark
- Luke

- John
- Acts
- Romans
- 1 Corinthians
- 2 Corinthians
- Galatians
- Ephesians
- Philippians
- Colossians and Philemon
- 1–2 Thessalonians
- 1–2 Timothy and Titus
- Hebrews
- James
- 1–2 Peter and Jude
- 1–3 John
- Revelation

crossway.org/knowingthebible